Prai
CHAPSTICK EATER

"Jackie makes everyone whose life she touches, better. Her kindness and goodness resembles that of Mister Rogers. In so few words, with simply actions and energy, she's taught me a great deal about how to live and treat others. She also just so happens to be one of the funnest (this non-word is fitting in context), goofiest, quirkiest, enlightening people you could ever hope to meet. Her words, in person and on the page, will make you laugh, cry, and cry from laughing."

—**CHARLIE BRENNEMAN**, former UFC fighter, current motivational speaker, former roommate; current friend

"Jackie DellaTorre is the most inspirational human being walking this planet. Not just for what she overcame, but for how she shows up for others. Her kindness, generosity, weirdness, and selfless commitment to others is so unique and endearing. This book is hilarious, weird, fun, sad, and inspiring; ALL at the same time. I love her, and I am so proud to be a part of her journey."

—**STEVE WEATHERFORD**, 10-year NFL veteran, fitness and motivation expert and Jackie's best friend

"Jackie DellaTorre has always been like a sister to Jionni and if you want to know the kind of person she is, then we are here to tell you about her. Although she does what she can to embarrass herself (and us) by dressing like like a hot mess for the church at our wedding, or when she farts and still blames it on Jionni's dog (that died 10 years ago), we still love her so much and know she will always be here for us unconditionally. We are very proud of Jackie for authoring her first book and we hope you love it as much as we do."

—**JIONNI AND NICOLE "SNOOKI" LaVALLE**, entrepreneurs; reality show personalities; Jackie's fake brother and fake sister-in-law

"Jackie is my very first Granddaughter and I have watched her grow from a beautiful little girl to a beautiful, talented, smart, and caring woman. She is our go-to girl who is full of kindness and joy for everyone (especially me). I am so proud of her debut as an author."

—LORRAINE RINALDI,
retired Rockette; Jackie's grandma

CHAPSTICK™
EATER

EXPLOITS OF
AN ODDBALL

Jaclyn DellaTorre

This book is dedicated to my brother, Neil.
Neil,
I love you, and I don't know what I'd ever do without you.
Also, I'm sorry I used to steal your Champion
sweatshirts and then get food stains on them.
Love,
Meat Back

Me in my beautiful dance recital costume, 1993.

Contents

Introduction

I know what those of you who know me personally are thinking: "Jackie wrote a *book*? She barely graduated high school."

You are right to question this. Let me be clear here: I have no idea what I'm doing. And not just with this book, but also in most aspects of my life. I'm an admitted scatterbrain and free spirit. The fact that I wrote a book isn't just hilarious to those who know and love me; it makes me laugh, too.

The birth of *ChapStick Eater* came from being the kind of person that outlandish things regularly happen to. All of my friends would constantly say, "Only you, Jackie," and "You should write a book!" As every new misadventure unfolded, my friends and I would all shake our heads in disbelief. Once I became a hairdresser, I used many of these wacky experiences as icebreakers when talking to my clients. They would say the same thing to me—"You could write a book!"

So I did. I started typing my stories into the Notes section on my iPhone. I had minimal ambition to actually write a book, but, for some reason, I just kept typing away on my tiny phone keyboard. It was a way to keep my thoughts organized, and to have something funny to go back and read when I was having a bad day. After a while, though, I realized the stories were adding up, so I started researching how to organize them into...something. Maybe a blog? Or maybe just a weird Instagram page? I didn't believe in myself enough to write a book at first, but after about a year, I realized, *Holy crap, I have a whole lot of notes!*

(Fun fact: I wrote 100 percent of this book on my iPhone and iPad.)

These short stories about my life are meant to entertain you with my weirdo antics and awkward moments. My hope is that, while you read this silly book, it will encourage all of you to laugh at yourselves and to help you find your "inner Jackie"— whether you're embracing your quirks, ruining your diet, sneaking food into your room to avoid being judged by your family, or embarrassing yourself by eating entire jars of pickles that don't belong to you. Let's face it: life's short, pickles are delicious, and you should be proud of that inner Jackie.

A note to all those related to me, whether through blood or not, who may feel nervous that I'll embarrass you: you should have behaved better. I'm sorry, I love you, and I hope you still love me after you finish reading *ChapStick Eater: Exploits of an Oddball.*

ChapStick Eater

There are people in this world who spend every day of their lives marching to the beat of a drum no one else can hear. You know the type of people I'm talking about—the square pegs in the round holes. The ones who pull on doors that are labeled clearly with PUSH. The ones whose socks have never matched—and will never match—a day in their lives. The ones who, in any given situation, feel like either the third wheel or the leftover.

For these, shall we say, wackos, ordinary tasks, such as planning or keeping things organized, give them hives. Fart jokes and potty humor will completely cripple them into cackling fits that normal people can't understand. For these sorts of characters, daily language is not so much "language" as it is an endless string of movie quotes. And, as if having memorized every line from a movie isn't enough, this breed of special square pegs will then watch that movie again and again, giggling louder every single time (and, of course, louder than normal people do the *first* time they watch it).

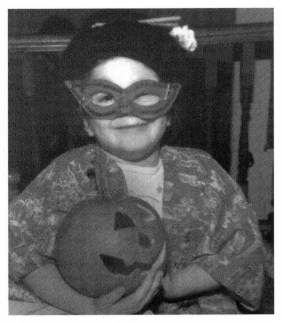

Me on Halloween, 1986. Yes, I've always been weird.

I think you know the kind of people I mean.

I am one of those people. Although I don't have the conventional life that includes a husband, a house with a picket fence, two kids, and a dog—the kind of life I'm sure my family wishes I had—I am content with the haywire life that has chosen *me*. Fitting in has never been my thing. While I have waded through periods in which I tried to blend in with the rest of the world around me, luck has never been on my side.

From the start, I was an oddball. As a child, I didn't just have stuffed animals. I had stuffed animals that had first, middle, and last names. I also had full conversations with them daily (before, you know, leaving them to converse among themselves). When I was in first grade, my teacher had to call my mom to pick me up

3rd grade Christmas play (They literally asked the chubby kid to play an elephant).

from school—not because of anything that was happening in the present day, but because I was too emotionally distraught over the day's history lesson (the assassination of Dr. Martin Luther King Jr.) to stop disrupting the class with my hysterical sobbing. I have no idea why this affected me so deeply, but my entire family talked about it for weeks. They all looked at me like I was a freak and wondered how a six-year-old could be that weirdly socially aware. To this day, I still am moved by the amazing stories of MLK Jr., but it makes me laugh out loud thinking about how odd my six-year-old self's reaction must have seemed to my teacher, parents, and extended family.

From the ages of two to six, I ate full tubes of ChapStick on the regular—forcing that gook down my throat until it forced its way back up again. Why my parents didn't stop me, I don't know. Maybe they thought it was funny. And, since I have always been a laughter hoarder, maybe that's why I kept doing it. Also, it was delicious, let's be honest.

The summer before second grade, I decided to be a badass and do what the cool big kids were doing: jumping into the town pool off of the lifeguard stand. Unfortunately, I did it in the shallow end. After I leaped into the water, things unfolded pretty much as gracefully as can be expected. I panicked, landed much sooner than anticipated, smashed my toes into the bottom of the pool, and broke four toes total—two on each foot.

I learned quickly that there's nothing you can do for broken toes; you just have to let them heal. So my dad taped up my toes, and I hobbled around in my brother's flip-flops all summer because my swollen toes wouldn't fit in my own. I can still remember limping around trying to keep up with my friends on the playground, using my twirling baton as a cane.

My pinkie fingers on both hands are crooked like question marks. They have been that way since I was born. When I started piano lessons at the age of seven, I went to bed every night with tape around my fingers, hoping that, when I woke up in the morning, they would be straight. In this fantastic dream of mine, my tape endeavor would be a rousing success, and I would suddenly transform into a gifted piano player with gloriously straight fingers.

I tried using every kind of tape I could find in my house (because the fact I was using the wrong *type* of tape was clearly the problem here). Scotch tape, duct tape, electrical tape…I even cut Popsicle sticks to make them into short, half-assed splints. I would then attach the Popsicle sticks to my fingers with medical tape, trying to force my fingers to bend into more normal-looking ones. Finally, my mom realized what I was doing and had a fit. Once she caught on, she checked my pinkies every night after I had fallen asleep to make sure I had stopped taping. Her (logical) fear was that I would cut off the circulation and make my problem of crooked pinkies into an even bigger problem in the future, such as nerve damage or blood flow issues.

I can't imagine there are many parents who check their sleeping children's fingers for tape each night.

From the age of eight until about 16, I thought I wanted to be a teacher for children who are deaf. I have no idea what first gave me the idea, but I used to *beg* my mom to buy me books about sign language, and I always *insisted* on watching TV with the closed captions on (and volume off). Unsurprisingly, this drove my entire family crazy. They constantly searched for the remote to take the never-ending stream of words off of the bottom of the television.

Once I came to the realization that, if I became a hairdresser instead of a special needs teacher, I wouldn't need to go to college, I eventually abandoned the teaching idea altogether. However, as a fringe benefit of my years of practice and preparation, I did become an excellent lip-reader. Now, when I blow-dry my clients' hair and can't hear what they're saying to me, I still know exactly what they're saying. A completely bizarre childhood habit became an extremely useful adult skill set.

I have always had lots of loyal friends with whom I could always have a blast, act like an idiot, drink too much, and do "normal" things the cool kids did. But truthfully, as a teenager I was most at home when I was knitting a scarf or playing rummy 500 with my grandma. I was basically born a nana who liked to party once in a while. As a young person, I was embarrassed about this and tried to hide the fact that my craft collection was more important to me than fancy purses or cool clothes. I pretended I wanted to be the girl with the brand-name accessories instead of the girl who dreamt about Mod Podging anything within reach. Crafts and old lady things aside, though, my one true love in life is getting a laugh—at any and all costs.

One of my earliest memories is of my father sitting next to my four-year-old self on our old couch. We were watching early Saturday morning cartoons before the sun (or anyone else in our house, for that matter) was up. Before I could stop it from happening, a fart snuck out. I felt my face get hot—maybe because I sensed it was an embarrassing thing to do, but probably because I figured I was going to get in trouble. To my surprise, when I looked up at my father, tears were pouring out of his eyes. He was literally convulsing because he thought it was the *funniest* thing I had ever done. That feeling of making him laugh was all it took to instill in me a desire to make everyone I knew laugh like that whether I meant to or not for as long as I shall live.

My brother Neil and I in 1986, I look thrilled.

Under the Rug

I held my breath and, as quietly as possible, I slid the package of Pop-Tarts into the waistband of my sweatpants. My father, Neil, was working at his night job. My stepmother, Lynn, was unsurprisingly half-drunk-half-asleep in her bed at 7:00 p.m. on a Friday night. Walking as slowly and carefully as possible to avoid waking her up, I crept past her bedroom door. If Lynn were to be stirred awake, she would force me to make her a cocktail, which would unnecessarily delay my long-awaited Pop-Tart feast.

Each step up the squeaky wooden stairs to my bedroom felt like an eternity. Then, finally, in the safety of my room with my door closed, I sat on the floor and opened the wrapper as stealthily as possible. From that moment on, I was in frosted-brown-sugar-cinnamon-Pop-Tart heaven. As always, I stuffed the evidence into a place where no one would ever find it.

It was 1993. I was a four-foot-eight tall 12-year-old that looked like a 50-year-old because I weighed easily 180 pounds. My clothes were either hand-me-downs from my adult aunts or clothes I bought at Bradley's using money I had earned babysitting for my neighbors.

My best friend since birth, Faith And I at my dad and
Lynn's wedding. Faith wore a sensible business suit.

My mom had died two years earlier, and my dad worked very hard at a couple of different jobs to pay all of our bills. My stepmother gobbled down pills, lay in bed, and rang a bell to summon my 16-year-old brother or me to make her frozen mudslides in the blender, pour her a glass of Pinot Grigio, or prepare whatever vodka concoction she could come up with. Who waited on her depended on who would answer first; or, if my brother and I were near each other, we would quietly fight until one of us gave in and went into her room to see what she needed. At the time, my brother was a cool teenager who spent most of his time at wrestling practice or out with his friends.

My life mostly consisted of walking to see my neighbors, the LaValle family, at their house or begging my best friend, Faith, to let me hide at her house—to feel like I was part of a normal family. When I wasn't at either of their houses, I was hiding in my own bedroom, eating my feelings away: I wolfed down any kind of candy I could find, plus Pop-Tarts, Ring Dings, Hostess apple pies, and anything else that could fit down my 12-year-old throat. In fact, I can't remember a time between the ages of 12 and 19 when I wasn't swallowing my emotions with a heaping tablespoon of vanilla icing out of the container or an entire sleeve of Oreos dipped in peanut butter. I had never wanted to burden anyone with my problems or tell anyone I needed emotional support after being through a lot of trauma at such a young age. I always pretended to be fine. So instead of talking to someone about my struggles, as a normal person would have, I just ate. Eating made me happy: it made me feel as if I was in control of something in my life, at a time when everything else seemed chaotic and out of whack.

My "fake family" L to R
Big Joe, Janelle, Jionni, Janis, my mom Patty, me,
James, Joseph, and Neil, my dad was taking the
picture. Atlantic City 1990

My mornings, on the other hand, were a different story altogether: without fail, they started with my dad waking me up at 6:00 a.m. to weigh me because I was on my "diet of the month." I can still hear him saying, "Why the frig are you getting so fat, Jackie?! You eat literally nothing! Maybe we should go to the doctor!" He didn't realize that the disgusting pre-packaged freeze-dried-then-rehydrated diet foods, like the microwavable turkey burger on a spongy bun or the disgusting poached fish, that he had ordered for me from Nutrisystem—and forced me to eat—were merely an appetizer to the delectable, post-bedtime treats I snuck into my room undetected. It was a real head-scratcher for my well-meaning dad, who only saw microscopic-sized portions of food entering my body and, as a result, could not for the life of him figure out why the scale kept going up. I promised him I would try harder and for that moment I really meant it. With an "Okay, Jackie. I love you, kid," he went to work for the day.

Why couldn't I have just become a slutty teenager or have started smoking pot like other kids from dysfunctional homes?

Fast-forward 11 years: I was now living with another one of my best friends Lauren in our own apartment, where I had been for about a year. My dad called to inform me that he was selling the home I grew up in, and that he and Lynn were moving to Fort Myers, Florida, as soon as possible. It was a hard fact for me to accept. Although I was older, a little wiser, and a little thinner at this point, being overly sentimental and attached to things that reminded me of my mom was definitely an emotional hurdle I hadn't yet figured out. I had come a long way from my binge-eating days, though. I had become a semi-functioning adult who, switching gears, had progressed from eating her feelings away to drinking them away. Ironically, I now barely ate, as did most of the 23-year-olds in my life at the time. That wasn't any healthier, I know, but I was still grateful to no longer be a big fat 12-year-old who ate herself into a sugar coma every night.

I wasn't dealing with the house being sold very well, and I will always feel terrible that Lauren had to deal with the crying fits and excessive drinking that characterized my life during this weird, traumatic time. She handled it like a champ and drank right along with me. We had more parties, played more beer

Lynn, me sweating like a pig in my 8th grade dance dress, and Neil going to his junior year prom, 1994.

pong, and watched more silly movies than anyone I knew—just to try and get my mind off of being sad for a little while. For that I will always be grateful to her. But at the end of the day, my brother was the only one who truly understood how heartbroken I actually was because he was upset, too, and he knew I associated the house with my mom's memory. I always felt nostalgic in our house, almost as if I could still hear my mom singing along to the radio as she stood at the sink while I helped her do the dishes, or as if I could still hear her hollering at my brother and me to move our asses every morning to catch the bus on time. It was as if every corner of our old house had memories of her in them. To me, at that time, it felt as if the house was all I had left of my mom. Whether that was a sane way to think or not was not my main concern at the time.

One night, soon after my father broke the news that he was getting rid of the house, I met up with my brother, Neil, for dinner after work. We went to our uncle Bobby's pub, The Half Point. It was a real-life version of *Cheers*. Everyone literally knew everyone's name, and it was our favorite place to go. While we were sitting at our table waiting for our dinners to come, my cell phone rang. It was my dad. He uttered only one syllable, yet I could already tell he was insanely pissed.

"Are you frigging kidding me, Jackie?!" he yelled. "There are enough wrappers under here to fill the goddamn Grand Canyon!"

He was screaming in his loudest "mad Dad" voice, which he reserved for moments exactly like this one. Tears instantly ran down my face as I tried to stifle my laughter. I knew EXACTLY what he was talking about, and I felt a combination of shame and embarrassment, mixed with sheer amusement, as my dad rattled on and on. I even put the phone on speaker so that my brother didn't have to miss out on this moment.

Although we never had officially discussed it, I was 99 percent sure Neil knew the secret I was trying to keep all of those years. Our rooms were right next to each other our entire childhood. No matter how much practice I had opening Pop-Tart cellophane wrappers, and no matter how hard I tried to muffle the noise, it was inevitable that the late-night crackling and crunching wouldn't have escaped Neil's earshot. Being the awesome big brother he is, though, he had never mentioned it or ratted me out.

Thrilled at my 8th grade graduation.

As Neil listened to my dad yell at me as if I were a child, he suddenly started laughing so hard that he was nearly dry heaving. Meanwhile, Big Neil hollered at top volume, "ALL THOSE GODDAMN EXPENSIVE DIETS I PUT YOU ON? AND YOU WERE EATING EVERYTHING IN THE HOUSE? DID YOU SERIOUSLY THINK I WAS NEVER GOING TO PULL UP THE AREA RUG? THERE ARE AT LEAST THREE THOUSAND WRAPPERS UNDER THERE!!!"

Neil and I could no longer control ourselves or our laughter: snot ran down my face, and Neil pounded his fist on the table uncontrollably. My dad continued screaming and said, "Are you two assholes seriously laughing this hard? What the hell is wrong with you?"

Frustrated and annoyed over our hysterics, my dad eventually hung up. While my dad fumed (presumably while standing over a pile of wrappers), my brother and I keeled over in laughter, and everyone else in the restaurant continued to stare at us blankly.

Apparently, stuffing my fat-girl evidence under my huge area rug wasn't as foolproof as my prepubescent brain thought it was. In the very back of my mind, I must have thought there was a possibility this would happen one day. *I'll clean it all up before anyone finds it*, I must have told myself a million times. But then, just as quickly as my life went haywire after my mom passed away and my father got remarried, so too did my life change just as abruptly when I developed a social life in high school.

So, I had just let myself forget about it. After all of those years of eating treats and hiding wrappers, I dropped my habit in favor of new habits: going to the movies, sneaking booze with my friends, and trying the best I could to be "cool." Sure, I still ate as much as two adult men could have eaten, but I wasn't doing it behind closed doors anymore. I moved out years later without ever thinking twice about the rug and what was underneath it. Until the very moment my dad called, I had just about completely blocked that gross collection of plastic wrappers out of my memory.

In the span of a single five-minute phone call, I felt terrible my dad had to clean that mess up, embarrassed he found it, amazed it took so long for him to find it, and honestly, as I listened to my dad scream at me, instantly starving thinking about all of those delicious feelings I had eaten to make that giant pile of garbage.

Ancestry.not

My father, a.k.a. Big Neil, is not a real person. I mean, he *technically* is. But, after spending just a little time with him, you'd quickly become convinced he's actually a sitcom character. Think of an Italian version of Kramer from *Seinfeld*, and you've got my father. Anyone who meets Big Neil is instantly obsessed with him and his quirks. He loves to draw attention to himself, usually by overexaggerating his Italian heritage, overplaying his role as a northern New Jerseyan transplanted to southern Florida, and going overboard with his devotion to the New York Yankees and New York Giants. He is one of the few people in his gated community who supports the Yankees and Giants; for the most part, the place is overrun by rival Boston Red Sox and New England Patriots fans. Despite this fact, or maybe *because* of it, my father insists on having the largest and most obnoxious New York team flags swinging from the flagpole in front of his house. Even his golf cart is decked out in Yankees' pinstripes: he relishes any attention—good or bad—he gets for it.

My dad is handsome with dark olive skin and hair that's perfectly in place. He is always impeccably dressed: I swear, I don't think I've seen a wrinkle on anything he's ever worn. Every single day, whether he is working in the yard or going to a wedding, he is always dressed to the T. God forbid he is seen in something less-than-perfect, like an untucked shirt. The mere thought of that would absolutely horrify him.

Where he lives in Fort Myers, Florida, he is one of the youngest guys in the retirement community, and, basically, he is hot stuff. He has all of his hair *and* all of his teeth, *and* he can still drive after dark. He needs nothing more to qualify as the hottest commodity in town.

Like most hot commodities, my dad is not lacking in confidence. He often comments on his own good looks, and he is usually convinced that most ladies he encounters are either flirting with him or have a crush on him. He even had business cards printed with his phone number and email address on them. His explanation: "I'm just too frigging popular down here, Jackie. I can't spend all that time constantly giving people my number. My life is way easier now with these cards."

All jokes aside, my father is one of the hardest workers I have ever known. He has never been afraid to take on more than most people could handle, whether it was for his family's needs or for his own needs. Big Neil is ridiculously handy. Taught by his mother, he can install Sheetrock, spackle, tile, do plumbing work, and handle literally anything in and around any house. If something needs improving or fixing, he can do it himself, and it will always look professionally done.

If there is a happier morning person than my dad, I would be curious to meet them. I don't know anyone else who wakes up and immediately starts singing every single day. His dream is to hang on to being an '80s guido forever and to grow out his "guido mullet." I'm a hairdresser by trade, so I certainly won't allow him to start traipsing around with some crazy-looking combination of long, curly hair in the back and short hair slicked-back in the front. Hilariously, his guido-mullet dream is the main thing we fight about when we see each other. His argument to me is that his hair is his identity. And mine is that he must be joking.

Like many of Big Neil's other over-the-top obsessions, his fascination with being a Leo is out of control. Versace himself probably would have gone to my father for tips accessorizing and decorating. The master bathroom in Big Neil's home is adorned with golden lion heads on every wall. He even wears a 24-karat gold lion head pendant with a diamond eye around his neck.

Big Neil's biggest source of pride is a shrine he keeps at home. The shrine is, for all intents and purposes, of himself. The shrine actually does contain a cool collection of mementos, including memorabilia from exciting events my dad has attended and

Big Neil. In all his glory.
(Note the gold lion head necklace.)

pictures he's taken with celebrities. In fact, the montage would probably even pass as normal—if my father hadn't also plastered the shrine with solo shots of himself. When Big Neil thinks he looks particularly stunning in a picture, that photo immediately makes its way into his esteemed collage of self-admiration. If you were to visit his house, the first thing he'd do would be to lead you straight to the Big Neil Shrine to contemplate its beauty. It is a place of constantly evolving self-worship, and it gets larger and more intricate every passing week.

Although Big Neil isn't fat, he can eat more than any human I know. To prove his talent at high-volume eating, he will actually randomly challenge the younger guys in our family to prove their manhood by making them eat an entire pizza with a hot dog for dessert, and wash all of that down with a pitcher of beer. In one sitting. Most of them puke it up, which he claims discredits their manliness test. His own claim to fame is that he once won a hot-dog-eating competition by devouring 17 hot dogs and 17 buns with only one can of soda. If he had a picture of himself winning that contest, it would undoubtedly have been blown up to life-size and positioned as the focal point of his shrine. After all, what's the point of having a shrine if it doesn't let you revel in the glory of your greatest life accomplishments?

One recent summer, Big Neil got totally sucked in by the Ancestry.com commercials on television. In true Big Neil fashion, he decided to get his DNA tested to see exactly where his ancestors came from. Although there was no doubt that both of his parents are Italian *and* that both sets of their parents moved here directly from Italy, he insisted upon ordering the kit, swabbing his cheek, sending in the sample, and waiting for weeks for the results. Almost a month later, after much eager anticipation, he received an email with the verdict. When he called me with the news, I was on a train into New York City with my aunt (and his sister) Adele to go see a Broadway play.

"I have something pretty serious to talk to you about," he said as soon as I answered. He sounded so intense. From the quiet, monotonous tone of his voice, which is not his usual upbeat tone, I could sense he was nervous. With slow, painstaking deliberation, he finally revealed the Ancestry.com results he had been waiting patiently for: he was from northern Africa and the Iberian Peninsula.

Then, his voice changed instantly. With downright excitement (and complete earnestness), he exclaimed, "Jackie, this makes so much sense! I have this beautiful, dark skin and these amazing legs. You remember what a fast runner Neil was when he was on the high school track team? I can't believe this is happening, but it really makes me finally understand a lot of things that never added up to us being Italian."

I considered the fact that, while my father is a very dark-skinned Italian man, my brother and I are as pale as the moon. *If this is true,* I said to myself, *then I'm a little pissed. If I am partly African and partly from the Iberian Peninsula, why can't I get even the tiniest bit of tan on my skin?*

While I was 99 percent certain it was just a mix-up with the website, nothing I said could change Big Neil's mind at that moment. My father truly believed he was African. Attempting to muffle my laughter, I told my dad I was sure it was just a mistake. After all, how could both of his sets of grandparents *and* his parents be so confused about their family tree for their entire lives? I recommended he contact the site—just to make sure.

But, Big Neil wouldn't hear it. Sternly, my father told me I was wrong. In fact, he was going to do some research on the areas where our ancestors came from. To top it all off, when I told my aunt the story, she was as enthralled by the news as my dad was.

Big Neil and I, 1983.

"Jackie, this is so astounding!" she exclaimed. "You know, I have always been so drawn to African culture! I can't believe this!"

There wasn't one ounce of doubt in her voice either. Although they both will never admit this, my father and my aunt are very similar. They're both easily swayed and *very* passionate about what they believe in. When my father and my aunt have made up their minds, nothing—not even a simple blunder by a company that promotes itself on afternoon TV—can get in the way. I tried to explain to my aunt that it was just a website and that the company could, theoretically, tell people anything it wanted to. But, just like her brother, my aunt was dead set on exploring the thrills and excitements of her newfound heritage. Positively giddy, she seemed ready to hug every African-American person she saw walking along the streets of New York City. During the course of the entire day, Adele was nearly floating on the polluted air around us, dreaming about the newly discovered blood pumping through her veins. It was all she could think about and talk about. She even went as far as to tell one of our cab drivers about our possible newfound heritage.

After a long but fun day, we were homeward bound on the train. Unexpectedly, my phone rang again. Once again, it was Big Neil, but this time he sounded different. There was an air of defeat in his voice, and I could tell he wanted to speak as fast as he could. Apparently, as it turns out, daughters can be pretty intuitive. In what can effectively be considered Ancestry. com's forced return policy, an apologetic follow-up email from Ancestry.com took back our northern-African-Iberian-Peninsular heritage. There had, in fact, been a mix-up with the results. Ancestry.com was, however, pleased to inform us of its next well-researched determination of our ancestry: a very surprising combination of mostly-Italian-and-a-tiny-bit-Eastern-European descent.

I think I forgot to mention that Big Neil hates to be wrong.

Completely miffed that I had been right, Big Neil huffily told me to "save it" just as I began to say, "I told you so." Left with no other defense, Big Neil reminded me that, *no matter what the results said,* I shouldn't forget he is still handsome and that his legs are still amazing.

Okay.

Thanks, Dad.

I won't.

Camping in Hell

The spring of seventh grade in 1993 was the grossest time of my life. My main hobby for the past two years had been eating my feelings away, so, at that point, I was really fat. Fat—and getting increasingly sweatier and smellier by the minute. My father had been remarried for a full year to my pill-popping, chain-smoking, alcohol-swilling stepmother when we got a letter sent home asking for volunteers to come on the seventh grade camping trip to Stokes State Forest, a state park in New Jersey. Without a second thought, I left the form on the table so my dad could sign the permission slip and I could bring it back in to my teacher. The next morning I quickly grabbed the permission slip, stuffed it into my backpack, and jumped on the bus. It wasn't until I sat down in homeroom and our teacher asked us to pass up our slips that I took mine out and uncrumpled it.

It was like the world was crashing down around me. I stared at my permission slip in horror: Lynn, not my father, had filled it out. Not only did she sign the permission slip, she also signed herself up to be a chaperone. A *chaperone*. I hadn't thought for one second that Lynn might want to come. Had I even suspected it, I certainly never would have left the flyer conspicuously on the table.

Seriously, why the *fuck* would she want to come?

I started to hyperventilate. Desperate thoughts began racing through my brain. I thought about telling my teacher I lost the sheet and asking her for a new one that I could secretly have my dad sign. But I didn't even have a chance to put my plan into action before the person in front of me swiped the form off of my desk, catapulting me over the edge into a hell that would last for three days.

The following week, we were set to go on our trip. My friends could sense my dread and tried to distract me as we left on the bus to the campground. When we pulled up on the bus, I could see Lynn, who had driven herself, attempting—but failing—to hide out of sight as she smoked a cigarette behind a narrow tree. I prayed no one else could see her, but of course that was short-lived. The entire bus saw her smoking and went nuts laughing. I got off the bus, walked over to Lynn, and begged her to please not to smoke on this trip. She told me to lighten up.

Faith and I at Stokes State Forest.

To get to our cabins, we had to trudge up a pretty steep hill, dragging our bags behind us. I did whatever I could to separate myself from Lynn, so I walked as fast as my chubby legs could carry me. Halfway up the hill, I heard someone hacking behind me. Naturally, it was Lynn, the avid chain-smoker. Only a quarter of the way up the hill at this point, Lynn was stopping frequently to cough and use her inhaler. My friends all roared again with laughter: they knew she couldn't breathe because she smoked two packs a day. Pretending not to notice her repeated stops, I kept walking right up the hill and straight into the most crowded side of my assigned cabin. Quickly hatching a plot to get Lynn as far away from me as possible, I pleaded with girls I had never even spoken to in my life to sleep in the beds nearest to me, so that Lynn and I would end up on opposite sides of the room.

Was my whole weekend going to be like this?

Later that night, every student walked down to the cafeteria to eat dinner and watch a live show about animals. I finally started letting myself have fun, and Lynn was behaving the best she knew how to. Always an avid animal lover, Lynn grinned from ear to ear as they brought out one cute fuzzy animal after another. In fact, she was one of the first to pet each one. *Maybe this wasn't such a disaster after all,* I told myself. And then it happened. The man giving the presentation brought out a humongous, hairy tarantula. From across the room, I heard Lynn scream, "Get that fucking thing away from me!"

The entire room went silent. If she had only squealed in fright, everyone probably would have understood. But my pill-popping, chain-smoking, alcohol-swilling stepmother had just screamed the word "fuck" to a room of 120 seventh graders.

No one knew what to do, and I tried hard not to start crying in embarrassment. The presenter luckily didn't miss a beat and went on with the show. Soon everyone seemed to forget it happened—or at least pretended to for my benefit.

The second day was better. Lynn and I were actually having fun together for maybe the first time ever. It seemed odd but surprisingly okay.

I should have known it wouldn't last.

A bunch of my guy friends started fooling around and tossing sticks at each other. After one accidentally hit Lynn's leg, she hollered at them, and the one who had thrown the stick muttered under his breath that she was a bitch. That was all Lynn had to hear. Between being stuck in the woods and being (undoubtedly) in withdrawal from not drinking, Lynn was not someone to mess with in her state. Grabbing the kid by the arm, she dragged him over to a teacher and forced him to tell the teacher what he had just called her. To make matters worse for my social life, the principal actually made him write her an apology letter when we returned back to school.

From that point on, she was the enemy—not just my enemy, but the enemy of most of the seventh grade. Her official name became "the bitch," and I just wanted to die.

On the third and final day, my stomach was killing me. Scared I was going to be sick, I told a teacher I needed to go to the bathroom. She walked me over to an outhouse-ish building. Because I am a wuss who is afraid of camping, the woods, animals, and bugs, I also convinced her to let my best friend since birth, Faith, come with me. I went into a rickety wooden stall with my flashlight and, when I looked down at my underwear, I saw something brownish.

Did I shit my pants? I thought for a split second.

Then, it hit me, and I immediately started getting upset. *I had just gotten my first period.* I began crying hysterically. I had never wished my mom were alive more than I did at that moment. Faith, thankfully, had already gotten her period and, like an old pro, had brought pads with her on our trip just in case. She told me she would walk to get me one.

I waited until I knew she was gone, and then I started cursing loudly: "Are you mother fucking kidding me? I'm stuck in the goddamn woods with my asshole stepmother and this has to happen? Fuck!"

I was getting it all out when my friend came back into the bathroom and handed me the wrapped sanitary pad (as well as a few extras) under the door. After I calmed down, I begged her not to tell anyone I had gotten my period. I couldn't be the girl with the foul-mouthed, chain-smoking, bitchy stepmother *and* the girl who got her first period on a school camping trip. As we walked back to join everyone else, Faith promised me she wouldn't tell.

I sat with the crowd and, despite how distracting it was, tried to pretend I didn't have a pad the size of a freaking mattress between my legs. Lynn asked where I had gone, so I told her I had to poop and left it at that. My period was none of her business.

Our camping trip from hell (mercifully) ended later that afternoon. As soon as I got home, I immediately went into my dad and Lynn's bathroom to steal whatever feminine products I could find. I definitely wasn't going to *ask* for any—I didn't need them knowing that I had started my menses.

Somehow, I managed to get by a full year without telling them about my period. Janis, my neighbor and my mom stand-in, who had also been one of my mom's best friends, helped get me sanitary products, as did my middle school health teacher, Mrs.

Francis. Mrs. Francis, bless her heart, would buy them for me and then leave them in a place in her office where I could always grab them if I needed them.

One day, over a year later, my father noticed a wrapper in the trash in his bathroom and told Lynn. She thought it was my first time getting it and decided to buy me a ceramic rabbit statue to celebrate. I was nearly a high school student by the time they noticed, so I'm not even sure what my plan had been at that point. Would I have just pretended forever that I had never gotten my period?

I'll never know because, instead, Lynn got to hand her almost high-school-age stepdaughter a white ceramic rabbit statue with a nipple pink–colored nose and say, with a cigarette hanging out of her mouth, "You're a woman now."

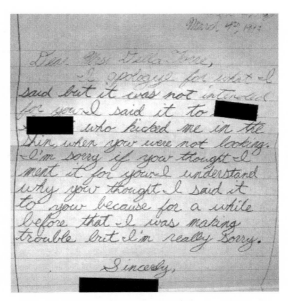

The infamous letter Lynn received for ratting out my classmate on the camping trip.

Disney World or Bust

When I was 10, my mom died. She had struggled with heart trouble for about eight years before it finally got her. She faced her health struggles admirably, and with so much courage and strength, that you never would have known she was sick. Unless she was having heart surgery or staying in the hospital, there were always meals on the table for our family. She never missed a day of work. She would run miles a day trying to get her heart to pass her next stress test—as if fixing her heart were up to *her*. She showed determination and fortitude throughout it all.

Losing my mom was, and still is, one of the most defining moments of my life. From the minute my father told me she was gone, I knew that, from that day on, I could only depend on myself. It may seem like a bold decision for a kid to make, but my father had been fully dependent on my mother. She had done *everything* for him. Once my mother was gone, I figured out quickly that Big Neil was not prepared for life as a single dad. He had to learn from scratch how to do laundry at the age of 39. He didn't know how to make any kind of food at all. In the beginning, we lived on pasta and on any food my extended family members would drop off for us; they knew my dad was struggling emotionally (and in every other way), so I'll always be grateful they stepped in for us. I will never fault my dad—he really did try his hardest, even though he was clueless about how to care for us and keep the house in order. He was unsure how to do laundry, let alone how to sort it by color, so my brother and I both wore pink underwear for a while, which didn't bother me, but my 14-year-old brother could have done without it.

After watching how hard it was for my father to adjust, I definitely knew I never wanted to have to depend on anyone other than myself. To this day, I still don't—for better or for worse. It's a curse to be so stubborn and to push everyone away, but I would rather be in charge of my own life, even if it means I make mistakes. Especially after watching my dad struggle because he was so dependent on my mom, I never want to put myself in that position.

A few months after we lost my mom, my father began dating one of my mother's friends. We had always called her "Aunt Lynn" but had only seen her about twice a year. Lynn was wild. At age 38, she was still a partier who would regularly go out drinking with her friends as if she were in college. She wasn't a terrible person, but, in retrospect, she wasn't someone who should have been around children.

A year later, my dad and Lynn got married. Just like that. I know my dad truly thought he was doing what was best for our family at the time. He was nervous about raising kids, especially a daughter, on his own, so his decision was likely the result of fear and desperation. Looking back, it was probably a mistake. My dad would even agree. At the time, he liked that she was the opposite of my mother. I think that, because she didn't remind him of my mom, it maybe made the transition less painful: my mom had been a homebody who lived for her family, and Lynn was still chugging wine and going to parties. He felt security in the fact that, even though he worked like a maniac, he wouldn't be leaving Neil and me at home alone.

After Lynn moved in, my brother and I knew our life as we had known it was over. And we were right. She was not kid-friendly. She didn't help us with our homework. She wasn't there for us when we were sick. She never worried about any household duties. If she was home, she was lounging lazily in her bed—eating crackers with butter and drinking Pinot Grigio (or whatever mixed vodka drink she was craving that week). Lynn would ring a bell for my brother (or me, if he wasn't available) to make her cocktails, so my brother essentially became a bartender at the age of 15. To this day, people often ask me why we didn't complain to our other family members, protest, or even just tell Lynn to go screw herself. I think it was because we were still in shock over our mom's sudden death; we didn't want to make my dad any more upset than he already was, so we were just complacent.

During the first year of Lynn and my dad's marriage, Lynn informed us we were going on vacation to Fort Myers, Florida, to visit her parents at their retirement community. It was exactly as you'd imagine a vacation to a retirement community would be. My brother and I spent the first day at the pool, with nothing to do but stare at elderly people strolling around in bikinis and Speedos. Their boobs were nearly around their waists (that went for the women *and* the men), yet these folks somehow had no idea their choice of pool attire was better suited for people a third of their age.

It was strange to see these retirees flirting with each other and slugging down drinks before noon. Their everyday life was like the kind of spring break college kids would dream about. To my brother and me, ages 15 and 11, it was mind-boggling. The only fun thing for us to do was ride around in golf carts, simply because being able to drive made us feel like adults. Other than that, there was nothing for us there. We couldn't drink. There weren't any other young people to meet. There wasn't even a mall nearby. We just baked in the Florida sun, watched adults in skimpy swimsuits get plastered, and prayed for the days to go by.

Halfway through our trip, it occurred to my brother and me that we were in the same state where Disney World was. We begged my father to take us there. ("Please, Dad, please! We can't look at any more saggy hooters. We want to go to Disney!" was among our desperate—and unsuccessful—pleas.)

My dad shot us down. "Are you nuts? Disney World is four or five hours away! We aren't going. Don't ask again."

Because we were good kids, we didn't ask again. And because there was no such thing as Google in the early '90s, we didn't know he was lying to us. Year after year, we would go back to Lynn's parents' country club—watching the old people act like they were in a college frat, and wishing Disney World weren't four or five long hours away.

Finally, a few years later, my dad informed us that we didn't have to go to Florida anymore (read: he and Lynn no longer *wanted* us to come). So, my brother and I were left home for a couple of weeks every summer. It was *awesome*. The minute Lynn and my dad left for the airport, our friends piled into the house. Our friends basically lived with us for a couple of weeks, and we threw parties every night. Everyone knew that Club D, as we called it, was open for business the first two weeks of every August. My brother and I had the time of our lives, especially knowing we didn't have to endure another awful Florida vacation.

Our friends were thankful our dad and stepmother were so carefree and didn't pay much attention to what we did. As soon as Club D opened, it was an animal house. When we would have our parties, our friends posed for pictures next to the poster-sized "Glamour Shot"—a photo of Lynn, with big hair and too much makeup, that she had hung on display in the house. (If you were around in the '80s and early '90s, you'll remember seeing a place in malls where you could have a "Glamour Shot" taken. If you weren't around then, I'll explain: for a hefty fee, an employee would do your hair and makeup in the gaudiest style imaginable. They would dress you up in feathered boas and sequined gowns, and then they'd take your picture as if you were a movie star. Instead of admitting she did this in the late '80s, Lynn told anyone who would listen that she was a model and that her friend who was a photographer had "asked to photograph her." Everyone knew the truth but just went along with Lynn's story to save her the embarrassment, I guess.) We played beer pong across the countertop in the kitchen. We even found Lynn's marijuana stash and smoked it. It was the perfect crime. There was no way Lynn would ever ask us where her pot went; doing so would be admitting she had pot in the house *and* that she smoked it. Knowing we'd get off totally scot-free, we never laughed harder than when we smoked that last joint.

I don't know if my dad didn't think we'd have parties, or if he just knew we were good kids who wouldn't let anything truly awful happen. To this day, I am remorseful that our neighbors had to endure our long, late, and loud parties—but thankful they never called the cops on us. There were times when they definitely should have. We got lucky that nothing terrible ever happened and that we were able to keep any creepy uninvited guests from crashing our bashes. It's kind of funny how much I've changed: as an adult, I would *hate* having young neighbors who threw ragers every night of the week.

Fast-forward 15 years to 2013. Big Neil was now a permanent Florida resident, living in the same gated community we used to visit all those years ago. My brother was married with two young sons, I lived on my own, and my stepmother had passed away from breast cancer just a few months earlier. My father was alone for the first time in his adult life.

We all decided to go to Disney World together—my brother, my brother's wife and kids, my sister-in-law's family, my dad, and me. Instead of letting my father drive four or five hours by himself to Orlando, I flew to Fort Myers the day before my brother and his family were due to fly to Orlando.

Big Neil and I woke up the next morning and got in the car to start our long drive. It was quiet for the first hour of the ride. I chalked it up to the fact my dad might have felt weird going on vacation so soon after Lynn had died. Less than another hour later, I started seeing signs for Orlando. It seemed strange, knowing Orlando was another few hours away, but I didn't think anything of it until my dad suddenly exited off the highway. Looking up, I saw a larger-than-life Walt Disney World: Where Dreams Come True sign stretching across the highway.

I looked over at my father in disbelief. As my father tried to stifle his laughter, tears poured down his face. I finally realized the truth.

Disney had never been four or five hours away, as he had told me so many times before. It was about two and a half hours away. In roughly just as much time as it would have taken for us to drive to Atlantic City from my hometown in northern New

Jersey, we could have gone to Disney from Fort Myers all those years. That son of a bitch had lied so many times, and I had believed him every single time.

Every. Last. Time.

Somehow, even 20 years later, he had still managed to dupe me. Even though I had an iPhone basically connected to my hand at all times at that point, I somehow had never once thought to look up how long the drive would take.

The first thing I did was call my brother, who had just landed at Orlando International Airport, and put him on speaker phone. When I informed him of Dad's lie, he was silent on the other end.

After a long pause, Neil finally said, "So we were tortured by having to stare at leathery, dangling boobs for all those years for no reason?"

My dad lost it. He nearly had to pull over from laughing so hard.

The gig may have finally been up 20 years later, but my dad had still won.

My Dad and I on our "long drive" to Disney World.

Cocktail Wieners

Whenever my father comes up from Florida to visit his friends and family in New Jersey, he stays with me. About 10 years ago he and Lynn came up for the Fourth of July. This was a holiday they rarely missed, probably because the day was always guaranteed to turn into an annual drinking fest for all of us.

Our town holds a yearly Fourth of July parade, and it is something that people who grew up here *refuse* to miss. Located in northern New Jersey, Florham Park is like a mix of a Norman Rockwell painting and the Jersey Shore. There are perfectly manicured houses with American flags displayed on impeccably kept lawns. Inside most of those homes live adorable Italian families—families who (like mine) proudly roam the town with their gaudy jewelry, amazing hair, and Italian flag reflectors stuck to their bumpers. On the Fourth of July, they fly their American flags higher than anywhere in the entire US. All of the residents (including me) are enthusiastic and proud, seemingly convinced our town's parade could compare to Macy's Thanksgiving Day parade. It can't. Yet, even though there's rarely anything more interesting than a bunch of fire engines and local politicians, we somehow always get caught up in the sentimentality of it all. It's that unexplainable nostalgia that keeps every single one of us coming back, every year, to cheer as if it's our first time seeing the parade.

As part of our yearly tradition, we start drinking Bloody Marys early in the morning (classy, I know). After the parade, everyone walks down to the local beer garden at the public park (yep, classy again). The beer garden is created in the park in the center of town for that one very special day. There you spend the day searching for your group of friends, catching up with old classmates, and dodging drunken creeps you don't want to get stuck talking to.

So, 10 years ago, my family arrived together at the park, and we instantly split up to meet up with our own crews. In my Bloody Mary haze, I managed to find my friends, and immediately joined them in drinking beer from a tap on a truck.

I was happiest to see my friend Dan there. Anytime we were together (and alcohol was involved), it seemed as if we couldn't stop ourselves from flirting. It also seemed inevitable that we were going to get together sooner rather than later.

Dan and I were inseparable that day: even as we caught up with our old friends and drank Coors Light out of huge plastic cups, we rarely left each other's side. In what seemed like the blink of an eye, the beer garden began emptying out, and my friends decided to go to a house party down the road. Dan and I followed the crowd, strolling arm in arm, laughing, and talking the entire walk. I can remember being so happy. After all, Dan was dreamy and funny—and he was one of my favorite people to spend time with. How could I *not* be happy?

From the second we arrived at the party, we couldn't stay away from each other: Dan spent most of that time trying to talk

Florham Park 4th of July parade, 2005 (ish).

me into sneaking upstairs into a bedroom. As drunk as I was, I still had my senses and didn't want to be disrespectful or get caught by anyone we knew while I was acting slutty. I preferred to go back to my place, so that's exactly what I suggested. I knew my dad and Lynn wouldn't be home until late anyway.

We caught a ride with a sober friend who dropped us off at my place. Dan immediately started kissing me as we walked in the door, telling me how happy he was that this was happening. All I could think of was how much I regretted my decision not to shave my legs that morning in the shower.

We beelined straight for my bedroom. As we jumped into my bed, something instinctively told me to lock the door. I quickly got up, locked it, and ran back to the bed, where Dan and I proceeded to act like two drunken idiots. We fumbled around clumsily and laughed, wanting nothing to get in the way of our fun.

That's when I heard it: the distinct sound of footsteps coming up the stairway to the front door of my condo.

Trying my best to not let the sound ruin the mood, I assured myself that it must be a neighbor. Dan noticed absolutely nothing. That is, until we both heard the unmistakable sound of jingling keys and a turning doorknob.

Suddenly, I no longer felt like a 25-year-old homeowner with houseguests who were out for the night; instead, I was like a drunk 16-year-old hiding a boy in my room from my father.

I could tell by the sound of their stumbling walks that they were wasted. My dad and Lynn were not the kind of people to ever leave a party early; in fact, they were typically the last man and woman standing at every event they went to. So, I told Dan not to worry—if they had left the party early, it must have been because they were too drunk to function. And, if they were as sauced as I thought they were, there was a good chance they'd pass out shortly anyway.

But Dan started freaking out. Because we had known each other for years, and Dan knew and respected my father, he didn't want to piss my dad off or make Big Neil hate him. He was panicked he'd look like a douche walking disheveled out of my room. I was also pretty petrified—despite the fact I was a mortgage-paying adult, had lived on my own for years, and had taken care of myself for most of my life, I was still nervous my dad would think I was a whore. Not to mention I felt terrible for Dan, who was so desperate to avoid an awkward situation that, at that point, in his drunken state, he was considering jumping out of my second-story bedroom window.

While we were busy planning out Dan's escape route, we heard Big Neil and Lynn shuffle into the guest room and shut the door. We paused and listened—all we heard was silence. As if a weight had suddenly been lifted off of our shoulders, Dan and I lay back down and began laughing hysterically at ourselves. We continued lying there, not really sure what to do. As long as we waited it out, we'd probably be fine…right?

Wrong.

Knock. Knock. Knock.

My heart stopped.

"Jackie?" my dad asked, pounding on the other side of my bedroom door. "Will you wake up? I want you to make me some of those cocktail wieners that are in the freezer!"

We froze. Obviously, I didn't answer. I waited and held my breath, hoping Big Neil would give up and return to his room.

But Big Neil was desperate to cure his alcohol munchies. He banged on my door again, his voice grew louder, and he whined, "Jackkk-ieee! Make me cocktail wieners! Please! I'm starving to death, and you have no food in this house!"

I felt as if my entire body had turned beet red from head to toe. I wanted to crawl under my bed and lie there. For-ev-er. I really thought I was going to die from embarrassment.

Big Neil was as relentless as ever. A master manipulator, he then said something he *knew* would make me get up: "Fine, I'll just drive your car to the diner."

Because I HATE when people drink and drive, he knew I'd do anything to keep him from getting behind the wheel—something we had had more than a few arguments over in the past. As he stood pounding on my door, I jumped up for fear he actually would try to drive. I quickly fixed myself up so I didn't look like I had been rolling around in my bed for the last half hour. Leaving Dan behind to get dressed in my room, I walked out and told my dad I'd make him his goddamn cocktail wieners *if* he promised to go right to bed and *if* he didn't try to drive anywhere. He agreed as he poured himself another huge glass of scotch and sat on the couch. After a few sips, he dozed off, as I had been praying he would. I put the hot dogs in the oven; then, I ran back to my room so that I could relieve Dan of his heart attack and lead him safely out my front door.

Just like that, it was over. I finally took a deep breath, thankful we had avoided an awful, awkward, intoxicated conversation.

Then, my phone rang.

It was Dan, who was wandering around in the parking lot in front of my condo and panicking yet again—he had left his ("fucking") shoes in my hallway, and his ride was coming, so he needed me to bring them out to him. Almost as if scripted, Big Neil woke up at the exact same moment. Drunk and still suffering from the munchies, Big Neil warned me in a dramatic tone that he needed to eat or else he was "going to pass away on [my] couch of malnutrition."

Big Neil had barely gotten the words out before he immediately passed back out on the couch.

Okay, Jackie. This is your window. Use it.

I opened my door, ran down the stairs, threw Dan his shoes, kissed him goodbye, and then scrambled back inside the house, which was now overcome by the smell of burning pigs in a blanket. I hurriedly pulled the hot dogs out of the oven and tossed them on a plate so Big Neil could enjoy his charred delicacy.

Sure enough, he did. Drunken Big Neil couldn't tell the difference between burnt wienies and normal ones. Robotically, he stood up, smothered mustard all over them, and chowed down on every last one—in under three minutes.

Then, with a "Love ya, kid! Goodnight," he went to bed to join Lynn, who had already been passed out for the past hour.

I wondered how much longer it would be before I heard another knock on my door.

Table Humper

Thirty years ago, my aunt pushed out a baby girl and brought home from the hospital my best friend. From the minute Mary was born, I treated her as my own personal doll. I have always been baby-obsessed—and that was no different when I was five. When my family would babysit her, I'd come up with unbelievably elaborate schemes to trick my mom into getting my cousin out of her playpen. I would climb a step stool and do anything I could—whether it was pulling Mary's bottle out of her mouth or pinching her—just to make her start crying. Each time, my mom would come running and scoop her up; thanks to the success of my well-thought-out plan, I'd get exactly what I had wanted all along: the chance to take a closer look at Mary and play with her.

Of course, as Mary got a little older and wiser, she would see me coming and, based on the years of pinching and bottle-snatching, she could easily predict what was about to happen. Trying to beat me to the punch, she would chuck her bottle right at me; those were the times we'd both end up crying.

To this very day she has the best and worst power over me. She knows exactly what to say to make me cripple with laughter,

Mary, Neil. and me, Easter 1987. There's definitely candy hidden in my purse.

and she can manipulate me so it happens at exactly the *worst* moment. Funerals, weddings, serious family events, church, or holidays, it doesn't matter. All she has to do is look at me a certain way or make a certain sound, and I break down immediately, with a stream of tears flowing from my eyes, snot pouring out of my nose, and an indescribable cackling filling the room. Even as a toddler—one who was five years younger than me, no less—she knew that, if she danced like a weirdo or ate something gross, she could make her goofy older cousin lose it. Our parents never seemed to know what to do with us. Honestly, even in our thirties, they still don't.

Three-year-old Mary developed strange habits. At any given moment, we'd catch her chewing on something wooden: our kitchen chairs; the pews in church; the bookshelf in our TV room; and her favorite object in the world, our coffee table. While the typical kid clings to a favorite doll, blanket, or toy, the not-so-typical Mary grew attached to a coffee table. She would lie next to it in sheer bliss, watching *Mary Poppins* (for the billionth time) and gnawing away like a beaver on the table's edges.

The table was made from bumpy '80s-looking light-colored wood and was shaped like an upside-down "U." It was a great source of fun for all of the kids in our family: the perfect shape to lie underneath, we would use it to hide from each other. (Personally, I also used it as a place to play with my Barbies in peace, without my brother trying to wrestle me or fart on me.)

But Mary, unlike the rest of us, wasn't interested in the nook underneath the table. Instead, she couldn't get enough of the table's very bumpy surface. After some time, she outgrew her habit of chomping on the wood. One day she decided to lie on top of the table and rub herself all over it. Since I was also a kid at the time, I had no understanding of what she was *actually* doing when she ran her body up and down the table. I just thought she was a fucking weirdo.

But, the adults in our family would snicker and then promptly tell her to "get down and stop that!" I didn't realize what Mary was actually doing until, as an adult, it hit me that she had been *humping* the coffee table.

As soon as the thought occurred to me, I could barely believe it. Did my three-year-old cousin really use our *coffee table* as her own gigantic bumpy sex toy? Needing some validation I immediately called my brother and asked him if he remembered Mary grinding on the table all those years ago. He chuckled and said, "You mean when she would dry hump it and moan when she was three? Yes. It was the oddest thing I had ever seen in my life."

The next time I saw Mary, I asked her if she remembered her table-humping days. The second I brought it up, it was as if my words smacked her directly in the mouth. She sat there in a strange daze for five minutes. Then, suddenly, she yelled, "Oh my fucking God! I forgot all about that! I didn't even realize I was using the table in that manner until you just reminded me. Do you think everyone realized what I was doing?"

I couldn't lie to her. As mortified as she was, I still told her that, yes, everyone either had already known or had eventually figured it out on their own. She said she could remember that bumpy table like it was yesterday. She credited those bumps for awakening her inner slut. Even at the age of three, she knew she liked that warm, fuzzy feeling she got from rubbing her vag all over my poor parents' coffee table.

Despite a childhood filled with peculiar wood-abuse habits, Mary still has become a very successful biochemist. She has many degrees and has worked in the fertility field, where she has helped hundreds, if not thousands, of couples conceive babies. Not only that, she also now manages labs across the country for one of top fertility clinics and tissue storage companies in the world. I'd highly doubt that there is a better-suited job for her than the one she already has.

She is the perfect mix of ingenious and hilarious: she keeps the facilities running smoothly and, with her quick-witted smart-ass mouth, she keeps things lively. She has a filthy sense of humor and can make the toughest truck driver blush with her quick, raunchy jokes (she has stopped openly humping wooden objects, though). The nature of her job provides her with material for jokes and humor; we do nothing but laugh when we catch up at least once or twice a week.

Hands down, the strangest phenomenon that surrounds Mary is the fact that people she barely knows—even perfect strangers—feel the need to insult her. Sometimes these unsolicited and offensive barbs get under her skin, and she ends up calling me crying. But, by the time we're done on the phone, we usually can barely remember why she was even upset. Luckily, we have the unique ability to turn the other's mood around and make each other laugh until we cry (or puke).

Classic example: Mary isn't fat at all. She's just an average American girl with huge hooters. But, for some reason, people always ask if she's pregnant, or when her baby is due—even though it's very clear she isn't expecting. At a family wake, an acquaintance started rubbing her belly and asked, "When is the blessing due?" Mary, who was already crying from an emotional week, actually had to explain to this rude person that she was "on a low carb diet and it clearly wasn't working." Moments later, when Mary told me this ridiculous story, I needed to excuse myself—and then so did she. Neither one of us could keep it together, and we didn't want to laugh at a wake.

We have never been able to figure out why anyone would say something like that to a woman. Unless a mother clearly states she is pregnant, I am a firm believer in not mentioning a pregnancy. Even if the baby bump seems obvious, people should hold their tongues until after the baby has crowned. Before that, just ignore the bulging stomach until further notice.

It is a true blessing being a Rinaldi. Rinaldi, as you can probably guess, is both Mary and my mom's maiden name.

We come from a tough stock and can take a (metaphorical) punch in the gut without getting upset. To the Rinaldis, laughter is the best medicine on both good days and bad days alike. Humor helps us to make the most out of rotten situations, especially the ones that life inevitably blindsides you with when you're least expecting. We can enjoy fat jokes in good fun, and, in trademark Rinaldi fashion, we find amusement in things that other folks would find demeaning or embarrassing.

Pickles and Cheese, Please!

At one point after I bought my condo, I decided that maybe I should get a roommate. While that had seemed like a great idea in theory, it turned out, in fact, to be slightly disastrous in practice. After my life was turned upside down by one very awful roommate who made the grossest mess of my house, I abandoned the roommate idea altogether.

Or so I thought.

To my surprise, just a year after my horrendous living situation had ended, a friend of my fake family, the LaValles, asked me if he could move in. Charlie was a former college roommate of James LaValle, one of my fake brothers, and over the years he had become close with James's entire family and me as well. At the time he inquired about becoming my roommate, Charlie was living in Pennsylvania, but was training as an MMA (mixed martial arts) fighter just minutes from my home in New Jersey. We had talked about living together a few times throughout the years, because he was always driving back and forth between northern Jersey and Pennsylvania for MMA training, but it wasn't until after Charlie was signed by the Ultimate Fighting Championship (UFC) in the fall of

2010 that he seriously asked me if he could move in to make his commute and life easier.

After thinking it over, I figured, what the hell? I already knew him and liked him as a person. I also already knew and liked his girlfriend, Amanda. And I was pretty sure that they, unlike Roommate #1, wouldn't be converting my condo into a pigpen.

So, I said yes. We all got along very well (thankfully), and our life became like a weird, hilarious sitcom, especially once they got married to each other and had a baby—while still living part-time in New Jersey with me.

As in most roommate situations, the politeness level during the first six months of living together was very high. Quickly (and fortunately) it became almost nonexistent—it didn't take us long to realize that we didn't care about looking gross, having zit cream on our faces, or farting in front of each other. In fact, we were soon perfectly *comfortable* doing all of those things in each other's company.

Not long after Charlie moved in, it was St. Patrick's Day. As we all know, whether you are Irish or not, St. Paddy's Day is a drinking holiday. After work that day, I went barhopping with my coworkers and drank enough beer to kill an army. After I got dropped off back home and stumbled into the kitchen, I saw a note from Charlie saying that he had gone back home to Pennsylvania for the weekend.

Now, I am notorious for never having any food in my house. As a chronic overeater, I don't trust myself at all, so I feel that not having food easily accessible is the best way to curb my appetite. Without much effort, I can overdo it on junk food. (And if junk food isn't available, I'm more than happy to overdo it on whatever healthful snacks are within arm's reach. I have eaten entire bags of grapes and whole watermelons, in case you're wondering.)

Basically, it doesn't matter what kind of food it is, I will over-eat it if given the chance.

This made living with Charlie slightly problematic—due to Charlie's intense training, he needed food constantly. And due to my equally intense eating habits, I needed to *avoid* food constantly.

So, back to the night in question—drunk and hungry, I found myself alone with a fully stocked fridge.

In my drunken state, I shuffled over to the fridge, where I found a brand-new package of Charlie's Kraft cheese singles (which I would never eat sober) and an entire jar of brand-new pickles. I removed both items from the fridge, sat down at the table, and ate everything ravenously. Every last plasticky slice of cheese and every delicious dill pickle made their way down my throat—one after another after another. Pleasantly stuffed, I drank a huge glass of water, took an Advil, and went to sleep even though it was only 9:00 p.m.

Let me tell you something: salty pickles and cheese do not do wonders for the body. When I woke up the next morning, my hands and feet were extremely swollen. In fact, all of my extremities looked like oven mitts. The beer, pickles, and synthetic cheese had wreaked havoc on my body, and I was so mad at myself. I spent the whole day drinking water, both to get rid of my hangover and to flush out the excess fluid from my limbs. My ridiculous (yet somewhat lofty) goal for that day was just to be able to fit shoes on my feet.

That night, Charlie returned to the condo because he had early training the following morning. As luck would have it, the first thing he did was walk into the kitchen and open the fridge so that he could snack on his new jar of pickles. My heart started pounding as the memory of my Saturday night binge session came rushing back.

"Jackie? Where are my pickles?"

Fuck.

"And my Kraft cheese singles?"

Fuck again.

If this had been a few months later when I was more at ease around him, I would have just told him the truth. But we were still in that annoyingly polite, honeymoon roommate phase, and I didn't want him to know (yet) how disgusting I actually was.

So, going instead with the first thing that popped into my head, I yelled back, "Oh crap! I owe you new ones! *All* of my coworkers came back here after we went out drinking, and *all* of us ate them!"

It was a white lie, but one that was necessary for the sake of my mental well-being at the time. The thought of Charlie calling all of his friends and family to tell them what a filthy animal his new roommate was—complete with details of how she ate an *entire* jar of pickles and polished off a huge package of Kraft singles on her own—made me want to jump into traffic. So, I lied. Actually, to this day, I still have never told him the truth.

A year later, Charlie, who was the picture of good health, had a stroke on my bathroom floor. At the time, neither one of us understood the severity of what was happening. We truly thought he was having a terrible episode of vertigo or a vicious stomach bug. Charlie was able to talk, and he told me not to call 911, so I didn't. In retrospect, it's now clear to me that his slurring, projectile vomiting, and profuse sweating were all signs of a stroke. But I unfortunately didn't put two and two together at the time.

After we opted not to call 911, we both somehow thought a better plan of action was to call my grandma. Within minutes, Lorraine walked in with Gatorade and some chicken soup—not exactly what the average hospital would recommend as critical to post-stroke recovery. My grandma helped me walk Charlie across the hall to a spare bedroom, where he stayed for the next week, not moving except when he needed to vomit or to be helped to the bathroom.

After that, every ounce of modesty left our friendship. You cannot help a sick man take a whiz without becoming close—and without becoming carefree about any other embarrassing thing that could happen when you live together. Eventually, Charlie was able to make it out of that guest bedroom, which we later lovingly named "The Stroke Room." He went to the doctor, where he was dealt what was probably the hardest news of his life. It wasn't until that point, three days later, that Charlie learned the truth of what had happened to him.

I'm sure Charlie's family hated my guts for not calling an ambulance. I still don't know why I listened to the sick, puking person who was lying in a pool of sweat on my floor and didn't just dial 911 instead. I will always feel guilty about not making the right decision at that moment. Reacting well during a stressful situation has unfortunately never been my strong suit, but, thankfully and most importantly, Charlie made a full recovery. In fact, the summer after his stroke, Charlie won the biggest fight of his UFC career.

Fortunately, Charlie never made me feel bad about it. We will always have a special bond (the type of bond that forms,

I guess, when two people clean up puke together—and try to treat a stroke with chicken soup). It also makes a great story because, not only was there a happy ending, but Charlie made it through that fiasco tougher than ever. Fingers crossed I'll never have to witness a stroke again—Lord knows I've proven I don't make the best choices during a medical crisis—and hopefully Charlie is never in that situation again either.

As a side note, Charlie, I am really sorry about your cheese and pickles! Those damn coworkers, though.

Jionni, Charlie, and I, 2011.

Wesley Snipes

In the summer of 2001, a bunch of my maniac friends and I started planning a trip to Las Vegas. I was finally turning 21 years old and I had felt like I had waited my whole life for this rite of passage. We decided that the beginning of November would be the perfect time to take on the Strip for our inaugural visit.

It felt like we had just booked our trip but then September 11, 2001, happened, and that was the day the whole world changed forever. Suddenly, things that once seemed normal, safe, and commonplace—even just days before—now appeared terrifying and threatening. Everyone, even the toughest men I knew, was scared of what was going to happen next. Our Vegas trip started to feel like it was a big mistake. By the time we were scheduled to leave for Vegas, I was feeling like a real jerk thinking about being drunk and partying, while the rubble piles where the Twin Towers had once stood were still huge and had hardly been moved yet. It felt as if it were too soon to fly anywhere. From across the Hudson River, we literally could still see the smoke rising from the crumbled buildings. All of us were seriously doubting our plan. Every horrible thought imaginable kept running through my mind: *Is it appropriate to be going to party in Vegas after such a sad, tragic event? Is it safe? Are we being disrespectful by going?*

My dad and I began discussing my concerns one morning before my upcoming trip. His classic Big Neil answer for me was this: "Are you friggin' kidding me? Go! If you stay here, then the terrorists win. That's what they want: for everyone in America to be scared. Screw them! Go have fun in Vegas."

I decided to listen to my dad, for once, and my friends all agreed. It was official: we were going. The time finally came, and we all got on the plane in Newark, New Jersey, with no problems and no drama. I had never flown that far of a distance before, but I was too excited to get there—and was so ready to see the sights—that I couldn't care or worry enough to be freaked out. About five hours later we got off the plane at Vegas's McCarran International Airport and walked through the terminal, making our way into the loudest, gaudiest, and most neon-emblazoned land. It was both awesome and offensive at the same time, between the signs for strip clubs on every other corner, the tourists with huge grins on their faces, and the drunk old men hitting on prostitutes. I loved it immediately.

Our nighttime drive from the airport was surreal: rows upon rows of gleaming lights illuminated every hotel and building within sight, and made it seem as if it were only noon. As we pulled up to our hotel and walked toward the front door, at least 10 little perverted men tried to capture our attention with their best howls and whistles. To their dismay, we were not enticed by their flyers advertising gross-looking prostitutes and strippers, and we continued on, ignoring them. We entered the lobby of the MGM Grand hotel, and it was A-mazing. Easily the most enormous and glittery hotel I had ever stepped foot in. As we rounded the corner to check in, there was a gigantic glass enclosure with two real lion cubs staring at us. It was surreal. It was the happiest, craziest place I had ever been, and we didn't have any issues with any asshole terrorists, thank God. We were blessed to have had four ridiculous days of gambling, drinking heavily, and sightseeing. If there is a more ridiculous place on earth than Las Vegas, I would love to see it.

Vegas had the best entertainment I've ever experienced. It had people from every walk of life strolling through its casinos— at all hours of the day. One minute there would be a group of men wearing bathing suits, visors, and sandals with socks, and in the next, a few women in the teeniest, tightest dresses would pass by in their six-inch high heels. I saw so many people in true pajamas (with *serious* bedhead) that it made me question whether they had woken up in the middle of the night to play the slots. Moms pushed their babies in strollers while drinking huge Long Island iced teas at 8:00 a.m. Men in business suits played penny slots, and people dressed in full costumes as if it were their daily attire. My favorite: a group of elderly women out celebrating their friend's 80th birthday could've easily been mistaken for drag queens.

In the midst of all of these outrageous characters, I decided to play a slot machine or two. I'm not usually a gambler. I work my big fat butt off for my money and feel weird about shoving it into a machine just to lose it. I would normally much rather drink or eat my money away, but today was different. I sat down next to a smelly old creep at a "Jackpot Party" slot machine. I shoved a $20 bill into the machine, pressed MAX BET a few times, and went through the money in less than a minute. I put in another $20. Again, nothing.

At this point I figured what the hell, when in Rome (or whatever that saying is), and put in a third $20. I pushed the button once and, just like that, what felt like every single light in goddamn Las Vegas shined down on me. The song "Macho Man" started blasting out of gigantic speakers around me, blaring at the loudest volume I had ever heard. I had won the jackpot, which was only $1,000, but you would've thought I had won a million dollars by the way this machine was acting.

Suddenly, I felt as if every set of eyes in the casino was on me. Because I'm a weirdo *and* was completely embarrassed *and* needed moral support, I stood up from my seat, turned beet red, and sprinted desperately into the crowd trying to find one of my friends. In my flustered haste, I abandoned the Jackpot Party machine—which was still screaming "Macho Man," by the way—for anyone to just walk up and swipe my winnings. Thank goodness my friend Lauren was around the corner and thinking clearly: she pushed me right back to collect my money while laughing at me for running away like the awkward weirdo I was. When I returned to the slot machine, the same crowd was still standing there waiting to see if I would come back or not. I'm sure they were also trying to figure out if something was actually wrong with me; insanity would at least give a jackpot winner a semi-reasonable excuse for nonsensically fleeing from her winning machine. My friends and I spent the night after my big win taking shots at a filthy dive bar, with everyone making fun of me in between each round.

After our binge-drinking fest, we struggled to wake up for what was my last morning in Vegas. It was the end of four wild days in Sin City and, with our hangovers and empty pockets, we all were more than ready to head home. We packed our stuff and

One of my best friends, Lauren and I in Las Vegas 2001

headed to the airport. Lauren and I had a nighttime flight, while the rest of our crew was leaving early the following morning.

For no reason at all, flying home felt different for me. I started to feel it in the cab on the way to the airport, but I figured it was just the result of a lack of sleep and the loss of brain cells from having chugged too much alcohol. During the flight out to Vegas from Newark, I was excited about the adventure of seeing a new place, so I was able to push any thoughts about terrorists or crashing planes out of my mind.

But, at the airport for our return flight, my palms began sweating, and my heartbeat was rapid as we walked through security. I told myself these were just signs of being dehydrated from having been drunk for four days straight. I made a mental note to get some water before we got onto the plane. Taking deep breaths, I paced around the terminal waiting for our boarding call. Our row was eventually announced, and I dragged myself onto the plane. After stepping through the door and onto the aircraft, I noticed Wesley Snipes, the actor, sitting in the last row of first class. As we passed him, my stomach dropped as I looked down at my boarding pass and realized that we were sitting only a few feet behind him in the first row of coach.

Now, a normal person would have been elated and would have thought, "How cool, a celebrity on my plane!" But, for some reason, it caused something awful to snap in my brain. As we took off, I started quietly crying. I have no idea why, but every negative thought that had ever crossed my mind during my whole life suddenly came rushing into my skull like a flood. At first I was trying not to draw attention to myself, so I closed my eyes and tried to pluck my dramatic thoughts out of my head as best I could. About an hour into the flight, I thought I felt a little better, so I opened the window shade to look out.

Opening that window shade ended up being my biggest mistake. By the age of 21, I hadn't flown very much, and what little flying I had done had never taken place at night. Flying was, in general, hardly a comfortable occasion for me. I was usually on edge during most flights. Not psychotically nervous—I was just the rosary-bead-praying-then-clap-when-we-are-landing kind of flyer. Suddenly though, this plane seemed like it was making louder-than-normal noises. And, by raising that window shade and suddenly being able to see the lights glowing on the ground below us, I managed to convince myself that I had never been able to see the ground this far into a flight before.

At that exact moment, I became a certifiably crazy lunatic. I started mentally telling myself that the only reason I could see the ground below was because something was wrong with the plane and the pilots wanted to be at a lower altitude to more easily attempt a crash landing. I repeated this to myself at least a thousand times in my head before I started actually crying out loud. And then, the thing I had been trying to avoid thinking and saying the entire flight finally took its hold over my mind: *Wesley Snipes is on this plane!*

In my warped mind I couldn't help repeatedly thinking, *Famous people always die in plane crashes. We are definitely going to crash. He was in that Passenger 57 movie about a plane, and that has to be an omen.*

That was it. Wesley Snipes had sealed my fate. Wesley, Lauren, and I were all going down together. I resigned myself to the fact that this was going to be our ending. Our friends and family would talk about it for years to come, telling each other the story of how we crashed and died with fucking Wesley Snipes and what a shame it was because he was such a good actor and he had been in that movie about a plane.

As the hours passed, dear Lauren, patient and easygoing Lauren, started to notice that I was freaking out. Lauren had been flying her whole life and, a very naturally calm person, she would never be scared on a flight. I tried to watch her, thinking her calm, cool, and collected demeanor might somehow rub off on me and calm me down. Yeah, that really didn't work.

She softly started to whisper to me that the reason we could see the ground was because the weather was great out and, in fact, it was *so clear* that we could even see some lights from the cities and towns below us. I didn't even let her finish before I began rattling off my theory that the plane was actually crashing. Of course, I didn't do this in a quiet, inside voice; instead, in my loudest, most obnoxious voice, I yelled, "We are fucking crashing, Lauren! Why else would we be so close to the ground? Wesley mother-fucking Snipes is on this plane, Laur! Famous people ALWAYS die in plane crashes! We are going down! FUCKING WESLEY SNIPES!"

At that moment, every passenger on the entire plane, including Wesley Snipes himself, started whispering and staring at me in horror. Poor Lauren was mortified and wanted nothing more than to crawl away from me, but the FASTEN SEAT BELT sign had just been illuminated to get us ready for our landing. She was stuck sitting next to me—trapped and miserable.

After I heard the landing gear drop into place and felt the plane begin descending, I started to calm down. I was finally able to take deep breaths again. Lauren was relieved this nightmare was almost all over—for both of us. She started nervously giggling over how ridiculous the entire flight had been. The minute we landed, I snapped out of it and started laughing at myself a little, too—but only for a minute. The dread of embarrassment quickly hit me like a ton of bricks. Every single traveler had heard my rant. I hardly cry in my regular daily life, so it made me want to puke thinking that I had not only cried in front of complete strangers, but that I also had sobbed and yelled in front of at least 200 people. I put my head down and followed Lauren off the plane as quickly as possible.

A few feet ahead of us, Wesley Snipes was also trying to exit. He turned and glanced (well, glared) at me. Wesley had one other person with him. Wesley leaned over to his friend and murmured something into his friend's ear. His friend quickly picked up his cell phone and spoke in a hurried whisper to whomever was on the other end of the line.

When we finally walked off of the plane and into the terminal, there was a group of security guards waiting there. It suddenly felt as if I was going to faint or shit my pants. I started sweating bullets at the thought that maybe I was getting arrested or, at the very least, committed to a mental institution for my not-so-Oscar-worthy performance on the flight. Instead, the security guards surrounded Wesley and guided him away from the crowd.

It took me a full 30 seconds to realize that they were guiding him away from me. *Specifically.*

The proof: he said something to the group of guards swarming around him, and, one by one, they all turned to look directly at me.

The best boss on earth and one of my best friends, Cathy D. and I.

Stool Samples and Blowouts

Let me start by saying I LOVE being a hairdresser. The owner of the salon that I have worked at my entire career, Cathy, is one of my best friends, and I am thankful to have her in my life. I have known Cathy D. (as I call her) since I was 12, and we have been through a lot together. One of our favorite topics to discuss is how, for some reason we haven't quite figured out, people love telling their hairdressers the very deepest secrets and most intimate details of their lives. At any given moment, a hairdresser can bounce back and forth between being a guidance counselor, a psychiatrist, a nurse, and even a priest waiting to hear confession. Luckily for my clients, I was born to be a good listener, and I always have been since I was a kid. Unluckily for me, I hear some personal and yucky things. And, for the sake of not hurting a client's feelings, I have to pretend they don't bother me.

I love my clients, even the grumpiest ones, with all of my heart, but they often put me in uncomfortable positions, whether or not they realize it. I've endured moments when I've been cutting a client's bangs and that woman has suddenly confessed, while we were basically nose-to-nose, that she had been throwing up the entire night before. (NBD, folks. She feels *fine* now.)

I've had countless customers look to me for a professional opinion on their maladies. News flash: My opinion that something looks more like a hive than a poisonous spider bite, or that a growth behind your ear looks more like a skin tag than a cancerous mass, does not constitute professional advice. Reason #1: I have less than zero medical knowledge. Reason #2: I barely made it out of high school. Yet, these people, these dear *adorable* people, skip off just as gleefully with the haphazard guesswork of Jackie DellaTorre, pseudo-M.D., as they would from a yearly visit with their general practitioner.

Our elderly clients are especially inclined to rattle off about their bodily occurrences or to force me to examine some icky thing that has grown on their skin. I've looked at—and been made to feel—many huge lumps on people's bodies. Clients have pressured me to give my opinions about their rashes and to check their tonsils for signs of strep throat, despite the fact that I have absolutely no experience (or desire) to do either.

It will always amaze me how free-spirited elderly people are with their nude bodies. Some of our ladies will shuffle in, lift up their shirts, and ask for help hooking their bra. Some will strip their shirts off right in the middle of our salon to put robes on. It doesn't matter if there are men or children around, things just get whipped off and tossed around with little warning. One of my favorite clients of all time, may she rest in peace, would often remind me that she hadn't worn a bra in years. Not that she even had to tell me. It was pretty hard to miss her long, mushy boobs swinging around wildly by the waistband of her pantsuit. Bless her heart.

Literally, by a mile though, my least favorite thing to hear about is my clients' bathroom habits. They tell us about how they've developed chronic diarrhea, how their food "has run right through them" since they had that colonoscopy, and how they haven't been able to poop the same since they went through their "changes." While I am someone who DEFINITELY finds potty humor hilarious, it is completely different to be told these stories dead seriously, with no joke intended, by my cute little customers. No matter how much I love all of them, it still turns my stomach.

One fateful late summer morning, we had a strange woman bring a medical sample into the shop. She was sitting in my coworker Jill's seat, waiting to have her hair done, when she suddenly jumped up, walked over to the coatrack, reached into her jacket pocket, grabbed a little jar covered in a clear plastic bag, and walked back over to us. She then placed the jar on the top of Jill's workstation (which is right next to mine) and sat back down in her seat. She didn't utter a word about what was packaged so neatly in that little jar. We assumed it was nothing out of the ordinary—people very often bring in home hair remedies for us to use on their heads (their friends recommended they try them, their daughters said they were amazing, blah blah blah). Jill and I just let it go for a little while; I, for one, actively tried to disregard what, in all honesty, looked like shit in the clear container. Actual excrement. But, after grimacing in the mirror at each other, Jill and I both clearly couldn't stop thinking about it. After trying to ignore it for about 20 minutes, I finally had to ask what it was.

I really wish I hadn't.

What I heard next would forever be burned into my mind. In the most horrible way.

"It's my stool sample," she said matter-of-factly.

"Ummmm, *what*?!" I replied.

"My stool sample," she repeated. "I'm going to the doctor after this and didn't want it to get warm in my coat pocket. Actually, can you refrigerate it for me?"

"NO! We can't. I'm very sorry, but that's disgusting and unsanitary. Our *lunches* are in there," I said bluntly.

She was not happy with my answer. She sat with a disapproving puss on her face for the remaining hour of her hair appointment, which felt like 100 years. All the while, the poop just sat there, making itself cozy on Jill's countertop. When she was done, she picked up the jar and left with a huff. There wasn't enough bleach in the world to disinfect Jill's station.

I have been told I have a certain "face": one that makes people feel comfortable. Apparently, it's a face that invites people to disclose their most disgusting thoughts and habits. One day last year, I realized how true this was. A frequent customer came in for her usual quick haircut. During many of her prior appointments, she had alluded to the fact she wasn't well and was trying her best to get better, but she had never clarified what was actually wrong with her. I am not a question-asker; I am a firm believer that people will tell me the things they want me to know. I think it's rude to pry, and, in a situation like this, I honestly am always a little frightened to hear what the answer will be.

On this fateful day, the woman began telling me about her terrible diarrhea and confessed that she couldn't "trust" any of her farts anymore. While she sat there—in earnest—rambling on and on about *trusting* her farts, I began to think, *Would the words "can't trust my farts" ever even leave my mouth? And, if they somehow were to, would I force someone I hardly knew—you know, like some poor person cutting my hair—to listen to them?* Bathroom humor makes me giggle, but this definitely was one step too far. I was so close to finishing her hair when she abruptly said, "I have to go to the restroom," and jumped up to go down the hall to use the bathroom. I waited for about 15 minutes until she shuffled back up front. As soon as she sat in my seat, the smell overwhelmed me like a fog of rotting death. I could only begin to imagine what had happened in our restroom. She asked me if I was done and then informed me very casually that she had "made a big mess" in our restroom. As I attempted to understand what she was telling me, her husband suddenly walked in to pick her up. Before I could react, he threw money on the desk and told me she called him from the bathroom—and then they both ran out.

My chair smelled like absolute garbage. I was freaking out as I cleaned it, and I tried not to vomit as I scrubbed it furiously with ammonia. It suddenly hit me, and everyone else in the salon at the time, that I needed to go check the bathroom. As I got about halfway down the hallway, the smell encased me. I did my best not to cry or hurl, but little did I know that the worst was coming. I walked into the bathroom and saw nothing but poop. Everywhere. It was like she pulled her pants down, pointed her asshole up in the air, and sprayed diarrhea all over the walls, floor, and toilet. After a volcano had erupted out of that woman's anus, she decided it was okay to relay that information as flippantly as she did, as if she were telling me that we ran out of toilet paper or that our soap dispenser was empty. "See ya, I sprayed poop everywhere. Byeee!" Then, she thought it was acceptable to just let me find it and to leave me to clean it up. I cursed her every minute of the cleanup. I hated her with all of my being. Every cell in my body wanted to rip her from limb to limb, but, instead, I told myself to woman up for the sake of the other clients and my coworkers. I walked back toward the bathroom, turned on an upbeat playlist on iTunes Radio, put on rubber gloves, and tried not to dry heave as I started wiping down the walls.

Luckily for all of us, she decided never to come back. While I would never usually say something like that about my clients, in this instance, I was extremely thankful I never saw her again.

Pull My Finger

My grandfather Mario Joseph DellaTorre (also known as "Moe," "Morris," "Mariuch," "Dad," or, what I called him, "Pop Pop") was one of the people I adored most—and definitely my comedic inspiration.

Pop Pop lived for compliments. An ardent self-admirer, Pop Pop consistently told people he was 10 years older than he actually was, just to get people to say how great he looked for his age. Until the day he died, he was convinced every woman he met was flirting with him; yet, even after over 60 years of marriage, he would get jealous at the drop of a hat if any man paid attention to my grandmother Tess. Neither of them were ever short of confidence, and Pop Pop always tried his best to keep up his appearance. He always begged everyone in our family to buy him self-tanners and hair dye but insisted we couldn't tell Grandma; he knew she didn't want him to look better than her, so he had to do it under the radar.

Pop Pop was the father of four and grandfather of 10, and every single one of us adored him. As a young man, he joined the Air Force during World War II, as did all five of his brothers. Pop told us stories of how he had guarded German prisoners of war as they were flown to where they would be held. He even said he would try to make the prisoners laugh because he felt bad for them. He knew many of them were just kids fighting for their country, just like he was; even though they were his enemy, he couldn't help but think of them also as human. He was the most accepting and loving person I knew. To him, there was no difference between people of different races, religions, or anything else.

After he came back from the war, he and my grandmother got married. As the story goes, he was asked to audition in New York City to become an actor. When a production company offered my grandfather a job, my grandmother had a fit, so Pop Pop turned it down to make her happy. They were ridiculously in love their whole lives, and he would have done anything to keep her from kicking his ass. After reconsidering life as an actor, Pop Pop went on to open his own printing press business in Madison, New Jersey.

With four kids to raise and lots of bills to pay, my grandfather got a second job at night as a security guard. He wasn't great at it. At the beginning, he fell asleep during most of the shifts he worked. To keep himself awake, he started writing a story he made up: it was about a mobster who, using a stolen ferryboat, robbed a New York City bank in order to fund a school back in Italy. Pop Pop actually turned it into a novel, which I sometimes see for sale on Amazon.com. It's called *With a Ferry Boat They Robbed the Bank, Italian Style*. Riotous, it was filled with potty humor and ridiculous situations—ones that only hilarious my grandfather could have thought of.

He struggled with alcoholism most of his adult life, but he willingly went in and out of rehab, motivated by the support of

My Pop Pop, Mario, the happiest nut I ever knew.

our family; even though it was hard on everyone, we knew in his heart he wanted to be better. Until the day he died, he would have given anything for a shot of vodka, and he would have been honest enough to tell you that right to your face. He knew he had faults, and he was the first to admit them. But he was still the most joyful person I knew, and the fact he could light up any room he entered was proof of that.

As an older man—which is how I remember him best—he called me at least once a day, usually to tell a joke or do something else to crack me up. Classic example: I always heard from him after doctors' appointments, because he'd call to say the female nurses at the doctor's office had been hitting on him. He'd say anything he could think of to make me giggle. Hands down, his favorite kinds of jokes were fart jokes. He was famous for the old "pull my finger" prank: he would hold out his finger for one of my cousins or for me to pull, and then he would rip a big, gross fart. Pop Pop would laugh so hard at himself that his eyes would tear up. It always amazed me: he never failed to have one that big waiting on deck.

Besides drinking, the other demon he fought was eating. He struggled constantly with his weight, and my grandmother tried her best to get him to lose some. Every week, she made a huge pot of tomato sauce with tons of meatballs in it. She would take out only a few meatballs for their dinner on Sunday and would give some to our family. Then, she always froze the rest, intending to dole out what she thought was an appropriate amount for him to eat every day for lunch or dinner. Cunning as he was, my grandfather would wake up before her, line his pockets with paper towels, head to the freezer, and put a couple of frozen meatballs in each pocket to defrost. The minute he could, he wolfed them down without my grandma knowing. He'd have a smile on his face all day, pleased to have pulled one over on her.

His other favorite food-bingeing trick was turning the ice cream container upside down, opening the bottom, and eating a little ice cream each night before putting the container back together. My grandmother, who had type 1 diabetes, didn't eat ice cream, so she never noticed the missing ice cream until she had company over for a family dinner, holiday, or birthday. When she would try to scoop some out, she would find it was hollow. Luckily for Pop Pop, since Grandma only ever realized it when we all were there to witness it, she wouldn't get as mad as she would have otherwise. Instead, we all just had a good laugh.

At my grandparents' house, one of the first things you would see was a huge calendar hanging up in the kitchen. My grandparents marked each day of the calendar with either "good BM" or "bad BM." After years of wondering what that meant, I finally asked my grandfather about it.

"When I wake up, the first thing I do is take a shit," he explained. "Then, I walk downstairs and write whether or not it was good or bad."

As often happens with our crazy family, I came to the conclusion that I probably shouldn't have asked.

From that point on, armed with that knowledge, all of us would shake our heads and chuckle about it. I'm sure that was part of the reason Pop Pop continued updating the calendar, too—he lived to amuse us and would do anything for a laugh.

One summer day Pop Pop, who was a devout Catholic, called his kids and a few grandkids to tell us he had a sign from God growing in his backyard.

"A pine tree grew into a cross!" he exclaimed. "This is the sign I've always been waiting for!"

None of us had ever heard him talk about waiting for a sign, but that didn't matter to Pop Pop—he immediately started building a shrine around the "holy" tree. He found a statue of the Virgin Mary, spray-painted the face of the statue gold, put a small altar by the tree, and adorned the area with rosary beads. Every day, he sat back there and prayed. Eventually poor Mary's face turned green from oxidation and the elements. The pine-tree cross became overgrown and unrecognizable, but Pop Pop just claimed that was a sign from God to keep going. The eternal optimist.

Besides being a gifted storyteller, my grandfather could sing wonderfully. He was *by far* his own biggest fan, though. He would start singing everywhere he went, just to show off his talent. At home, he had a huge karaoke machine, which he used to record himself singing, as well as reciting poetry he had written. He recorded several CDs of songs and poems; and of course, in true Pop Pop fashion, he couldn't resist the urge to throw in a few jokes between tracks.

Among the many recordings he had made was one CD we found when he died. It was labeled "play at my funeral." The recording started out with Pop Pop singing "My Way" by Frank Sinatra; before the Sinatra song got too sad, it quickly transitioned to Louis Prima's "Just a Gigolo" and "I Ain't Got Nobody" medley. Pop Pop ended the track by saying, "Hey! Don't be sad. I'm doing fine! Love you all. Over and out!" That ending—a nod to how he had ended every phone conversation he had ever had—couldn't have been more perfect. When we played it at his funeral, it made everyone smile between sobs.

A few summers before my grandfather passed away, I had given him a book called *The Story of Me* as a birthday present. The book asked personal questions about the reader's life and left blank spaces for the reader to leave his or her answers. At the time, Pop Pop had thanked me for it, but he never mentioned it to me again after that. I figured he had thought it was stupid and had just acted polite for kindness' sake. After Pop Pop passed away, though, my aunt Adele and I found the book in his desk drawer. To my surprise, it was completely filled out.

As I flipped through the pages, my heart was ready to explode. I was so happy as Aunt Adele and I sat together, reading it out loud. Our tears were mixed with laughter as we tried to make sense of Pop Pop's horrible grammar and spelling. My grandfather was one of the smartest people I knew—he could carry on political conversations as if he were running for state senator himself, and he could engage the brightest scholars in discussions about the arts and current events—but his grammar and spelling rivaled that of a grade schooler.

My favorite part of the book was his answer to the question, "Did you have any further education beyond high school?" His answer, verbatim: "the scool of hard kocks." My aunt could barely get the words out of her mouth as she read it aloud. We both hyperventilated with laughter, amused that, even from the grave, my grandfather could still make us laugh.

Pop Pop's uncanny ability to keep his audience entertained—whether he was writing a book, making music, or talking about "hard kocks"—lived on even when he couldn't.

Part of DellaTorre clan. Neil, Jen, Me, Uncle Lance, Aunt Adele, Aunt Dale, Uncle Mario, Uncle Guy, Aunt Jayne, Grandma Tess and Pop pop, Big Neil, Lynn, and Uncle Mario.

Leggings Were a Bad Choice

Growing up, my brother and I were blessed to have one of my mom's best friends live next door to us. Janis and her husband, Joe, had four children, which was awesome—among other great things, it meant we constantly had friends to play with. Then, after my mom passed away when I was 10, I started to basically live with them on and off, thanks to my dad's hectic work schedule. Part of the reason, too, was that my brother was older than me, so he was busy with teenager things and was never home. (Also, to be completely honest, I was probably just doing everything I could to hide from my wacky stepmother.) I consider all four of the LaValle kids my "fake siblings," and I couldn't be luckier to have them in my life. I'm sure my brother, Neil, would agree that having Janis; her husband, Joe; and their children as part of our "fake family" was a major part of what helped form us into the functioning, hardworking adults we have become. I am thankful every day for them, as well as for our grandparents, aunts, and everyone else who helped raise us.

When the youngest LaValle, Jionni, found his now-wife, we all got thrown into a tizzy. She is a famous reality-show star, whom he met during the filming of the show that made her famous. Since I am very overprotective of him, as most "big sisters" are of their younger siblings, I had plenty of reservations at the start of their relationship. She was a world-known figure with paparazzi following her day and night and, to be honest, at the time they met she was mostly known for acting wild, being drunk, and getting arrested. Jionni was "our Jionni" who every one of us babied and swooned over. The thought of him being on TV and involved with any drama or tabloid criticism seemed terrifying; I can't speak for anyone else, but I know I felt a little uneasy about what was going to happen next. (I'll never forget Janis's panicked call to me at work the first Saturday morning Nicole slept over—I can still hear Janis whisper-yelling that "the girl from that *Jersey Shore* show" was "upstairs sleeping in Jionni's room!") Thankfully, though, I was proven wrong after getting to know Nicole. Nicole has become a dear friend of mine, and she's also a wonderful mother and wife. Four years and two kids later, they decided to get married, and I couldn't have been happier for them.

At the time Jionni and Nicole decided to get married, I was 34 and had been a bridesmaid and maid of honor in more of my friends' weddings than I could count. In fact, I have probably been a guest at more weddings than anyone else I know. I have worn long dresses, short dresses, awful dresses, cute dresses, and ridiculous dresses. I know all the wedding basics *and* the unspoken rules—like just to smile and nod when a bride asks if I like the dress she chose. In fact, that's pretty much the key to a successful wedding: smile and nod.

(From what I hear, that's also the key to a successful marriage, too.)

With all that practice smiling and nodding, I felt prepared

for just about anything wedding-related to be thrown my way. That is, until Jionni and Nicole's big day.

After I watched them hectically plan and perfect every last detail of their wedding for months, the much-anticipated day finally came. They pretty much had an army for a bridal party, and they had invited well over 400 guests to their wedding. It was one of the most wonderfully elaborate weddings I had ever witnessed—or ever *will* witness—in my entire life.

About an hour before the church ceremony, I began having an intense internal debate with myself about what I should wear.

You're not in this wedding and no one is going to look at you, so you should just be comfortable at the church for a change... Yeah, just wear a nice formal coat—no one will notice you aren't dressed up yet. There is plenty of time to change into a dress between the church and reception... But, the entire wedding is being filmed for TV, and you don't want to look like an idiot if the cameras happen to catch you in the crowd...

After a ridiculous amount of back-and-forth, the part of my brain that wanted to be cozy won the battle. For the first time ever in my wedding-attending life, I decided it would be a good idea *not* to wear a dress to the church. I believe my exact final thought on the subject was something like this: *No one cares about what you're wearing, so just put on a smile and shut the hell up about it.*

As I walked into the church and checked in with the security guards who were confirming the guest list, I started to wholeheartedly regret my decision. Every other guest was decked out to the nines; meanwhile, there I was wearing black leggings, a long-sleeved T-shirt, brown leather boots, and a formal coat that I assured myself was long enough to cover my woefully inadequate outfit. My misgivings were shortly confirmed: as soon as I approached my family and friends, they all looked at me in unison with the same look of utter horror. Staring at my ugly outfit under my jacket, they started pointing to the wedding program. I glanced quickly over the program but didn't really grasp what was happening; that is, until Jionni's aunt Denise grabbed me by the arm and yelled, "What the fuck are you wearing? You're bringing up the gifts!"

If any of you have ever had a panic attack and have been overwhelmed with the sudden tunnel vision, hearing loss, cold sweats, fainting sensation, and nausea that accompany one, then you know *exactly* how I felt at that moment. (If you haven't, well, lucky you. Just try to imagine it.) Dread completely overtook me. I took deep breaths, trying not to puke—or shit my pants. I spent half of my time hating myself for my casual clothing choice, and the other half wanting to strangle Jionni and Nicole—all it would have taken was a simple "Hey, Jackie, all eyes in our enormous crowd of guests will be on you," and we could have avoided the humiliation of Dress-Like-a-Cowgirl-on-Her-Way-to-Yoga-Class Day.

In case you think I'm being melodramatic, I'll also take this opportunity to mention this: the crowd of guests not only was comprised of friends and family, but also the *entire production crew* for their show, *Snooki and Jwoww*. So, not only would I be embarrassed in front of everyone in the room, but audiences at home would be able to watch—and rewatch—my humiliating moment to their hearts' content. I immediately started praying that I'd be cut from the final episode.

The option of running home quickly to change was out of the question. Between the TV cameras, wires, and production staff everywhere, and the hundreds of guests stuffed into the church, I knew it wouldn't be easy to stealthily sneak out and then back in again. Just getting into the church parking lot had been a complete nightmare because of the paparazzi and fans who were lined up to get a picture of Nicole and Jionni. Leaving the lot and returning in time for the ceremony was a completely stupid idea, so I had to resign myself to the situation as it was: I had no choice but to take my coat off and prepare myself for the embarrassment to come.

I sat and nervously watched the minutes tick away until the ceremony started. The priest came over to tell me he would nod at me, as well as the other pre-chosen gift-bearers, when it was time to head to the back of the church to carry the gifts up.

Then, just like that, it started, and the clock began ticking down to my dreaded moment.

Completely consumed by my thoughts, I missed *everything* that happened at the beginning of the mass. Instead, I desperately tried to think of a way to make myself look better.

A scarf? No, that won't work.

I looked over at my friend sitting beside me and noticed that her earrings were bigger and sparklier than mine. I considered making her swap with me but then decided against it.

What about Jionni's grandma's fur coat? Never mind...too weird.

It took a while, but I finally resolved myself to the fact I looked like a loser, and there was nothing I could do about it. I tuned into the ceremony, and, at last, the dreaded signal came. The priest indicated for me to walk to the back of the church, and I dutifully trudged back there. Three of Nicole's friends greeted me, and I noticed they were dressed perfectly; apparently, *they* must have been well-informed of their wedding duties. As if the situation weren't bad enough, Nicole's friend Joey, dressed in a white tuxedo and made up with a full face of makeup, looked at me and said, "Wait, that's what you're wearing?"

Of all the things I needed to hear at that moment, that was *not* one of them.

I was convinced diarrhea would start dripping down my legs and into my boots at any moment. My friend Bob, who was equally as clueless about his gift-bearing role as I was, looked nervous, too; but, in dress pants, a nice shirt, and a tie, he was at least wearing something that resembled wedding attire. The same couldn't be said for my getup.

As I waited in misery, holding my plate of communion to carry up the aisle, I decided there was nothing else I could do but turn on my bridesmaid smile. After years of training and many treks up the aisle, my pretend-this-is-the-happiest-you-have-ever-been smile had been perfected for this very moment.

We got the signal from the priest to start walking, so I plastered the biggest, phoniest smile onto my face. As I passed by everyone who should have told me ahead of time that I'd be the center of attention for part of the day, I began imagining I was backhanding each and every one of their heads. That would have been a relatively small punishment, considering the price I was paying for their omission. Seriously, how hard would a "Jackie, you're walking the gifts up and all eyes will be on you for a short time at the wedding, so WEAR A GODDAMN DRESS!" have been?

I could have won an Oscar for how stupidly happy I pretended to be as I carried up that golden plate in my dumb outfit. As I approached the altar, I bowed to the crucifix over the altar like the well-prepared Catholic girl I am; then, I handed the plate to the priest and bowed again, all the while smiling like a freaking mannequin.

I sat down. My moment in the "sun" was over.

The only thing left to do was wait for the ceremony to end and the cameras to stop rolling. Only then could I be put fully out of my misery.

Jionni and Nicole at their wedding reception.
Fanciest. Wedding. Ever.

Jionni and Nicole's wedding, 2014.

Praying Hands

Life working in a salon is super hectic, fun, and full of wild maniacs at all times. Some days it's as if you walk into work, blink, and realize it's already the end of the day. Those are my favorite type of days. It means we worked hard, made money, and were able to talk to mostly lovely people all day. When it's all over, especially on a Saturday, there's a strange calm that settles over the shop. All of the stylists have chatted for the last nine or 10 hours until there is nothing more to speak about. At that point, we all just like to be quiet for a little while before we move on to the rest of our day.

One Saturday afternoon, the salon had cleared out for the day. All of the other stylists had left. Only our receptionist, Melissa, and I were left to close up. We both noticed that an elderly woman was parked in a parking spot right outside our front door for quite a while. We mentioned it to each other and then went about our business closing up the salon for the weekend.

After I cleaned up my mess from the day and Melissa shut down the computer, we again looked up and saw this little old lady. As we watched, her head slumped down until her chin was on her chest. Both Melissa and I are terrible in emergencies, and we started to freak out, fearing the worst. Just as we were headed to the door to get a closer look, this woman's head shot back up. For a second it looked as if she was going to put the car into drive and run us over, so we ran away from the glass door and plate glass windows. It turned out that she was just reaching over to change the radio station. After realizing how silly we were acting, we chuckled and again went back to our business.

A few more minutes went by and we noticed she was again slumped forward, this time with her head resting on the steering wheel. Growing concerned at this point, we decided to watch her for a little while. If she didn't move in a reasonable amount of time, we decided to go out and ask if she was okay. She didn't move for 10 full minutes. Like the two big babies Melissa and I are, neither of us could get up the nerve to go outside and check on her. What if she was dead? After the hellish workday I had just had, I was not prepared to see a dead person. It was an image I'd never be able to get out of my head—and I certainly wouldn't ever sleep again if I knew she had died as we were watching. Like me, Melissa was also freaked out at the thought of approaching a dead body. We were paralyzed by fear, but we also knew we had to do something.

After debating what to do, we decided to call the police station. We thought dialing 911 would be too dramatic, so we called the actual local station instead to see if they could send someone down to check on her. We immediately felt like jerks as the dispatcher on the other end of the line said, "I'm sending an officer down, but why don't you just go out there yourselves and check if she is okay?" We didn't have a great answer, just the truth: that we were fucking scaredy-cats who didn't want to see a corpse that close up. Seeing a relative's embalmed body at a wake is scary enough; the thought of examining a dead stranger was too much for us to handle. So we waited for the officer to come.

It felt as if we were waiting for an hour, but realistically it was only five minutes or so before the police cruiser pulled into the lot. As I hid my eyes, Melissa watched the scene unfold. She yelled a play-by-play so that I'd know what was happening.

"He's getting out of his car!"

"He's walking over to her car!"

"He's tapping on her window!"

"She isn't moving!"

"He's tapping again!"

"Oh my God! Jackie, she isn't moving!"

"I CAN'T BELIEVE SHE DIED!"

I uncovered my eyes slowly, feeling terrible we hadn't called sooner. We both stared in horror at what was transpiring in front of us.

The officer tapped on the window one more time. This time, much to our shock, the lady's head shot up. Relieved by this unexpected turn of events, we watched in amazement as she rolled down the window and began talking to the officer. The officer looked over at us with a strange look before he turned back to the woman, who was still speaking to him. After chatting with the officer for a few minutes, she put her window back up and pulled out of the parking lot. Just like that, she was out of our worried minds forever.

We were dumbfounded. If she had been alive that whole time, how the hell did she not hear him knocking on her window?

With a smirk on his face, the police officer came into the salon.

"You two are the ones that called that in?" he asked us with a chuckle in his voice. He clearly knew the answer to that, but we nodded in unison anyway.

"Well, she told me that she is on her way to her daughter's house for dinner, but she realized she was too early and didn't want her daughter to get annoyed with her," he said. "So she pulled into this lot to listen to the radio and pray on her rosary beads."

What could we say at that point? Jackie and Melissa to the rescue. In the name of the Father, the Son, and the Holy Spirit. Amen.

Did We Just Become Best Friends?

I am a five-foot-tall, pale, kind of chubby, average-looking hairdresser. Of my many talents and interests, not a single one is in any way related to sports. If you ever need a cross-stitched gift sewn for your grandma, a helping hand on an art project, or someone to hem your pants, I'm definitely the lady for you. But, if you need another person for your adult softball team or want a running buddy, don't bother even *looking* in my direction— unless, of course, you need my help finding someone else to do it. My complete lack of sports knowledge is rivaled only by my even greater lack of athletic ability.

Yet somehow, as the irony of life tends to go, one of my best friends is a former professional athlete.

In the summer of 2009, Steve Weatherford strolled into my salon to get a haircut and walked straight into my heart. For those who don't know who Steve is, he is an enormously tall, tan, and handsome former National Football League punter. He is the kind of guy with all of the athletic ability and confidence in the world. Essentially, he's the polar opposite of me.

The day Steve sat in my chair to get a haircut was the same day he signed his contract with the NFL's New York Jets. On that same fateful day, he informed me we were going to be best friends. Little did I know he actually meant it.

The Jets' practice facility is located in Florham Park, New Jersey. That also happens to be the same small town where my hair salon is located. Geographically speaking, becoming best friends was easy: I was always at work, and Steve stopped in to visit me any time he had a break.

The start of our friendship was like a scene straight out of the movie *Step Brothers*. In that scene, Brennan (played by Will Ferrell) asks Dale (John Reilly), "Did we just become best friends?" Dale responds, "Yup!" That was all it took for Dale and Brennan. And that was pretty much it for Steve and me.

When Steve introduces me to people as his best friend, I'm usually met by some blank stares. People are usually confused trying to figure out who I am and why I'm his best friend. I have had many people over the years think I'm either his personal assistant, the nanny to his children, or just some weirdo fan he brings around with him to various places. It always makes me giggle, honestly, because the contrast between us is hilarious. If you were to see us walking into a party, you would say we resemble Danny DeVito and Arnold Schwarzenegger from the movie *Twins*. Sure, Steve doesn't have Schwarzenegger's weird accent, and I have slightly better hair than DeVito, but the comparison is otherwise pretty accurate. In the movie, the character Schwarzenegger plays is a big tall muscle-bound specimen, while DeVito, who is at least a full foot shorter and not in shape at all, can make Schwarzenegger laugh anytime they're talking to each other.

All of those mismatched characteristics aside, we have a great friendship. We can make each other laugh until we cry. We're caring. We're silly. We have more fun dancing like weirdos, or riding around in his car singing to the radio, than anyone else I know.

Thankfully, Steve's wife, Laura, accepted me into their Weatherford circle (I'm sure after some careful examination of me). Steve and I have equally happy-go-lucky and wacky personalities that are well suited for our best-friendship; regardless, I have to imagine that, when Steve started telling Laura that this stumpy lady with glasses was his new best friend, she was probably thinking, "What the hell?" I'm sure that, after the first few times she spoke to me and realized I barely knew anything about football at all, she figured out that I wasn't the usual stalker-type NFL groupie. I am thankful to have found such a great friend in her also. Five Weatherford children later, I am Aunt Jackie to

Steve, my gigantic best friend and I.

all of them. I even had the honor of them surprising me by giving their fourth baby my name as her middle name. Josie Jaclyn came into the world on May 30, 2015, and she was (and is) perfect. Because the Weatherfords were in California when Laura gave birth, I was with them in spirit—*and* also via FaceTime, for most of her labor and pushing. (I know, we're sickos.) We hung up right before the actual "birth process," but then they FaceTimed me again the second before JJ let out her first cry. It was definitely one of the top three most special moments of my life.

Less than a week later, Steve needed to be back on the East Coast for minicamp with the New York Giants. I felt terrible for Laura and the kids that he had to leave them so soon after JJ was born, but I was also excited to see my best friend again.

Despite the fact that Steve has all of the confidence in the world, he still hates to go places by himself. Whenever possible, he prefers to have someone there with him to keep him company. I am always happy to tag along—I love wacky adventures, and spending time with my best friend pretty much guarantees one. Steve's calendar is constantly full of events, between his constant philanthropic work, the motivational speeches he gives to schools as well as Fortune 500 companies, his nearly weekly TV commentary appearances, his sponsorship-related commitments, and various fundraising events; Laura doesn't always have time (or energy) to go, especially because she's busy taking care of five very active little children full-time. So, sometimes my best friend duties include being his sidekick, which I love.

One of my all-time favorite adventures with Steve happened the week after JJ was born. When Steve came back home for Giants' minicamp, he let me know we were going to "some event at Yankee Stadium" on June 3. Because he had to be in the Bronx by 6:00 p.m., he told me to make sure I could leave work early enough to get to his condo in Hoboken on time.

At this point, many of the events we attend are so similar that, by virtue of the sheer number of them, they have started to feel repetitive. While many people would think it's cool to get a fancy gift bag or attend a four-course dinner at a fancy-schmancy restaurant, we've become slightly jaded. However, every once in a while, we get the chance to go to an event that totally surprises us. We really appreciate those events that make us exchange looks and say, "This is so fucking awesome!" That night was one of those times.

Steve and I at Yankee stadium, 2015.

After cutting hair all day in ripped jeans and flip-flops, I had no time to change my outfit before I needed to be in Hoboken to meet Steve. I doubted my attire big-time and hoped everyone else wouldn't be dressed up. Luckily, when Steve came walking out of his condo, he also had ripped jeans and sneakers on. In dressed-down solidarity, we high-fived and quickly left to head to the stadium.

We met up with Brad, our friend and one of Steve's business associates, and, as the three of us arrived that night, the stadium security guards pushed us directly into a crowded elevator. Moments later, we stepped into an area with a huge bar. The bar, which was surrounded by tables and overlooked the baseball field, was packed with tons of media personalities, sports stars past and present, and political figures. The atmosphere as we strolled around was pretty relaxed and friendly, as if a bunch of old friends were catching up with each other.

I have something called "imposter syndrome." Basically, it means I constantly feel as if I don't belong places, even if I actually do. I could be at a convention for short Italian hairdressers and still feel out of place. It's a pretty unexplainable feeling. Unless you also get these weird moments in which you have to give yourself a *goddamn pep talk* just to feel like you deserve to be wherever you are, you probably have no idea what I'm talking about.

My out-of-placeness on this specific night was not an imposter-syndrome moment. I truly, in no uncertain terms, did *not* belong at this particular event. I didn't have to look around very long before realized that, unlike *every single person* around me, I was not famous, athletic, rich, fancy, or any other word you'd use to describe these famous, athletic, rich, fancy people gathered in hordes around me. I also had no affiliation with the

New York City Police Department, which the event benefited, so I was out of luck there, too.

I wasn't able to fixate on this very long, as I soon heard Steve yell, "Hey! Where's my Jackie?!" When he finally spotted me standing in the crowd of huge sports stars and their gargantuan friends, he grabbed my arm and whipped me around toward the elevator again. As Steve and I rode it down a few floors to where the locker rooms were, Steve said he would be playing softball with a bunch of other celebrities against a team of NYPD officers. The event, WFAN's True Blue Celebrity Softball Game, was an NYPD fundraiser in memory of three NYPD officers who had been killed in the line of duty a few months earlier.

Steve and the other players headed into the locker room to put on their uniforms. Standing right outside the Yankees' locker room, I tried my hardest to blend in (even though I'd been largely unsuccessful at doing that so far all day). As Brad and I passed the time, casually leaning against the wall while we waited, a steady stream of people passed us by. I recognized former New Jersey governor Chris Christie walk by. He was followed by former Yankees manager Joe Torre, former Jets coach Rex Ryan, then-Jets coach Todd Bowles, former Mets manager Willie Randolph, former Yankees player Bernie Williams, then-Jets player Eric Decker, and sports commentator Boomer Esiason. Of course, I obviously didn't know most of these sports figures on my own. So they would have remained nameless-but-famous-looking strangers to me had Brad not been quietly telling me their names.

Finally, everyone was dressed and began piling out of the locker room. We followed the crowd through a kitchen and a bunch of winding stairways, which eventually led us right onto the field of Yankee Stadium. Even the least-sports-oriented per-

Me sneaking selfies in the Yankees dugout.

son alive (that would be me) could figure out this was a once-in-a-lifetime experience. *We were walking where the freaking New York Yankees played and practiced every day.*

As awesome as this feeling was, I couldn't help but feel guilty knowing how many people would die to be in my place. I decided not to take this moment for granted, and I stood in the middle of the mayhem, just taking in all in. I could imagine my father and brother freaking out if they had been there with me walking around the in field. I took as many pictures as I could so that I could remember everything and show Big Neil. (Big Neil, by the way, was at home waiting eagerly by the phone for me to text him some awesome shots so he could show them to his crew of friends at the pub he frequents.)

The game eventually started. I cheered like crazy from the dug-out while Steve went up to bat and ran around the bases with his teammates. When he wasn't participating, I tried to sit nonchalantly in the Yankees' dugout, pretending I wasn't feeling super-cool yet secretly taking selfies to send to my dad. Big Neil was in Florida, going wild over my surreal experience and over each amazing selfie.

The famous people playing only had to be on the field for a few innings each. After Steve's allotted time ended, we decided to head home. At the next break between innings, we gathered our belongings, said goodbye to our new friends, and made our way out of the dugout.

I took one last look around to savor the moment, know-ing this would probably be my one and only chance to be on the field at Yankee Stadium. Countless Yankees legends had set foot where I stood and had made history on this same field. Of course, sports fanatics (and probably even five-year-olds) would better be able to tell you about Yankees history than I can but even I understood the incredible opportunity I had been given to stand on that legendary field.

During the inning break, some of the celebrity softball players took turns speaking into a microphone about what the event meant to them. I looked to my right and there, standing in the middle of the infield, stuffed into his uniform, was Gov-ernor Chris Christie. In fact, despite how amazing the event was and how much money it raised for a great cause, the fundraiser unfortunately was largely overshadowed the next day by the press making fun of Governor Christie's gut, which had stuck out of his uniform the entire night.

As we were leaving, it was Governor Christie's turn to give a speech. He was not being received well by the crowd.

Governor Christie was very unpopular at the moment with local New Jersey police officers because of unfavorable changes he had been proposing to their benefits and pensions. He had also been embroiled in a big scandal ("Bridgegate") that had involved his staff closing the George Washington Bridge without warning in 2013. One of the major routes to Yankee Stadium is over the GW Bridge, so it was likely that many spectators had been directly affected by the Bridgegate closure and ensuing gridlock.

Those two things combined, it hardly seemed as if he had many fans there at all. As Governor Christie spoke he was heckled mercilessly, but he didn't even flinch. He talked with gusto, like a true, practiced politician. He seemed increasingly energized as he went on, almost as if he thought the crowd was cheering *for* him—and not booing *at* him—at the top of their lungs.

As we left, I followed Steve closely onto the field. I was trying hard not to lose sight of where he was going in this massive place. His legs are almost twice the length of mine, and he walks so much faster than I can. He wouldn't ever mean to leave me, but if I'm not paying attention, I could be suddenly 50 yards behind him. Also because I'm a self-conscious dork, I was a little nervous to walk across the field in front of the packed stadium. I was right next to Steve one second and, the next, I felt him pull away from me. In fact, he started *sprinting* away from me. I quickly realized he was running full speed, with his arms outstretched, directly at the governor. Governor Christie's security detail looked anxious and ready to pounce. Unfazed, Steve still charged right up to Governor Christie and wrapped his arms around the governor, bear-hugging him with all of his might.

Steve then grabbed the mic right out of Governor Christie's hands. Governor Christie still smiled, but he looked completely shocked. Steve, in typical Steve fashion, screamed into the mic, "GOOOO GIANTS!!! YEEEEEAH! COWBOYS *SUCKKKK*! WOOOHOO!"

The governor is a well-known Cowboys fan, which happens to be yet another reason why lots of people in the tri-state area dislike him. As Steve handed the mic back to Governor Christie, the governor shook his head. Thankfully, he still had that same grin on his face, so he seemed to be taking it lightheartedly—or at least pretending to.

Governor Christie tried to resume talking, but the crowd was howling too loudly at Steve's antics. Although Governor Christie was practically yelling at this point, it was virtually impossible to hear a word he was saying, even with the microphone. Meanwhile, Steve ran back over to me. He grabbed my arm and started running, dragging me behind him like a rag doll. We were laughing hysterically. As we tried to make a swift exit, I looked periodically over my shoulder to make sure the state police officers in Governor Christie's security detail weren't chasing us in an attempt to tackle Steve to the ground.

We finally made it to an exit, but the door was locked. Before we could make a clean escape, a state police officer briskly approached us, talking into a walkie-talkie. I expected him to have some strong words about Steve's performance or to reprimand Steve for having almost been tackled by multiple state troopers. Instead, he just smirked, told Steve what Steve had done was awesome, and opened the door for us without saying anything else. We laughed the entire way back to our car. This adventure, like many others with Steve, was unforgettable—and unlike anything most people could ever imagine. From the day he informed me we would be best friends, I had a feeling every moment I spent with him would be an adventure.

Desperate Times, Desperate Measures

Whenever something bizarre happens to me, it doesn't usually feel very funny at the time. It's normally an awful, awkward, disgusting, unbelievable, or unnatural situation—one that in retrospect is frigging hilarious but, at the time, is pretty much the opposite. To get through these uncomfortable situations, I usually have to remind myself that, when it is all over, at least I'll end up with a story that will make everyone cackle.

In the nearly 20 years I've been a hairstylist, many bizarre circumstances have helped fuel my addiction to getting laughs. I have encountered my fair share of oddities and mishaps.

One particularly memorable story happened with a longtime client, who, like some of my other elderly clients, eventually stopped living independently and visiting the salon on his own. A good man who had helped people in need his entire life, he was a pillar of his community and couldn't have treated me kinder over the years I knew him. As his health went downhill, he moved into an assisted living facility. I told him that I would come and cut his hair monthly, not just because I knew he was going to need it, but because I genuinely cared about him and considered him a friend.

Slowly, as the months passed, he got sicker and weaker. One week his nurse called and said, "Jackie, he had to have his leg amputated. An infection took over that they couldn't heal. Please come next month, though. He will need you."

So I listened. A month later, I paid him a visit. On my drive there, I tried to give myself a pep talk to prepare myself for what I might see. I tend to say dumb things—and make jokes that usually aren't funny—when I get nervous. My internal pep talk, a frequent occurrence in Jackieland, is always my desperate attempt to prevent myself from saying something mortifying—something that, in all likelihood, I'll inevitably blurt out anyway.

Prior to that day, I had never known anyone who had a limb removed. I have known people who were born that way or had limbs removed before I met them, but it had never been someone I was this close to. I didn't want to say or do anything to make him feel uncomfortable. In the past, letting myself over-think a situation like this usually led me to embarrass myself. To prepare myself for that day's visit, I started trying to predict what his leg would look like—while still hoping I'd be able to avoid an uncomfortable situation altogether.

I bet he will just have a blanket over his lap, and I won't even notice.

Just in case his leg was visible, I had a backup plan ready, too.
Just don't look down and don't ask any questions!

I was ready. As ready as I'd ever be anyway.

The elevator up to his room took what felt like a lifetime to get to his floor. Slowly, I walked down the hall and turned the knob of his door. There he was, with a big smile on his face. Sitting in his hospital bed, which had been moved into the living room, he wore gym shorts and a T-shirt. I walked over to give him a hug. Wasting no time and not realizing I already knew about his unfortunate situation, he said, "Well?" and pointed down to where his leg had once been. "This is my stump now; my leg is all gone," he added.

Basically given no choice but to glance down, I lowered my eyes. As he wiggled his residual limb at me, I felt all the blood in my body drain away. Since this was my first experience having someone close to me lose a limb and then show it to me (with a fresh scar) so soon after surgery, I couldn't help wishing I had said goodbye to his leg the last time I had seen him. This seemed like such a big loss, but there he was—still his usual happy self— showing off his residual limb. By our next visit, I had adjusted, but at that moment, I was trying hard not to look like I felt sorry for him and also trying not to faint thinking that my friend had needed such a serious surgery.

Then, I said the first thing that popped into my head— which, based on my track record, is rarely a good thing.

This time was no different.

"Welp, I guess you're a lot lighter now, huh?" I heard myself say.

My friend with one leg, his daughter who had come to visit him, a nurse, and an orderly who was delivering his breakfast all turned to look at me at once. I could hear crickets in the distance. No one laughed at my joke. No one humored me.

The sweat instantly started pouring out of me. Not one person uttered even a single word. I awkwardly stood there for a few minutes before deciding to get down to business.

Meanwhile, I wondered how the heck I'd cut his hair if he couldn't get out of bed. The nurse suggested turning him so his good leg would hang over the side of the bed and then propping him up from behind with pillows. His hospital bed was up in an

"L" position, so I thought that, by leaning his weight against that section of the bed, he could use that for leverage to try to hold himself up. After a lot of maneuvering by all of us, we were able to get him to sit up for about three minutes. After that, he kept slumping over, as his leg that was still there wasn't strong enough to help him balance on a soft bed.

I was there before my workday and had allotted myself an hour to get his haircut done, but it was taking much longer than I had expected. He was wobbling all over. Meanwhile, I was breathing deeply, trying not to have an anxiety attack because I was so worried he would fall out of bed and get hurt. I was afraid I'd let my friend down if I *couldn't* cut his hair and, selfishly, I was also anxious I'd be late for work. In a moment of panic, I decided to just grab the bull by the horns—I straddled his residual limb with my one leg on one side and my other knee on the other side, attempting to wedge him against the "L" of his hospital bed and keep him sitting up so I could finish his haircut. I ended up holding him up in that weird-looking wrestling move for almost 10 minutes before I finally finished cutting his hair. As I dismounted from his lap, I turned to see the entire room full of people looking at me with their jaws open. It looked as if they were trying to decide if I was a complete weirdo or a total genius. (Thankfully, my friend didn't even seem to notice. He was just so happy to have me there visiting him that he talked the whole time about his family.)

Back at the salon, I was met with similar expressions of horror when I recounted the morning's events. No one could believe I had straddled a poor old man and his amputated leg just to get to work on time.

You know what they say, desperate times call for desperate measures.

Or, in my case, every day calls for desperate measures.

G-Money

If you ever were to meet anyone in my family, especially on my mom's side of the family, you'd know from the first minute that we do everything in excess. We don't just eat, we gorge. Drinking isn't a casual experience to us; we drink until we can't stand. Board games, even just "casual" games of tic-tac-toe or Trivial Pursuit, aren't fun family activities—they are only played for blood and glory. We will debate you to the death about anything that is even the slightest bit interesting to us. Our days are filled with laughter, whether we're laughing until we cry or until we nearly pee in our pants. Sarcasm is more than just part of our language; it's second nature.

I'm sure that the main cause of our insanity is because there are so many of us—22 grandchildren, to be exact. This number doesn't even include significant others or the numerous great-grandkids that keep multiplying by the year. When we are all together, it's as if we burst at the seams with happiness: we truly can't keep our craziness tucked in. So, we choose instead to let it loose. We are, for the most part, obsessed with each other.

We only have one strict rule about our family, and all 22 grandkids follow it. We call it the "Rinaldi phone-call rule." The rule is simple: after 6:00 p.m., if any Rinaldi over the age of 50 (excluding our grandmother) calls us, we do not answer under any circumstances.

The rationale for the rule is equally as simple: odds are, those Rinaldis are probably drunk. They might at first *sound* sober, but it's just a trick. Their drunkenness will reveal itself about one minute into the conversation, and we have many years of experience to prove it. Some of us have lost hours of our lives—precious hours we can *never* get back—speaking to drunk relatives about things that only require a fraction of the time to discuss.

Part of the Rinaldi crew. Uncle Bobby, Stacey, Uncle Dave, Cousin Maddy, Cousin Elliot, Cousin Luke, Cousin Joe, Cousin Will, Cousin Rob, Cousin Mike, Cousin Livi, Cousin Justine, Aunt Kathy, Nephew Neil, Nephew Nick, Sister-in-law Jen, Neil, Me, Grandma.

To save myself and the ones I love so much, I came up with this rule when I was about 18 years old.

The rule has saved us countless times. Instead of answering those drunken calls, we let them go to voicemail without a thought. The funniest part is that all the "over-50s" are aware of the rule. They check their clocks, and, if it's after 6:00 p.m., they know they're supposed to text us if it's important. If the text is coherent enough, we will text back; if not, we will ignore all correspondence until morning. If they aren't sober enough to follow the basic rules, we don't put ourselves through the trauma of another belligerent talk.

As each younger grandchild gets old enough to be affected by the rule, the older, more seasoned grandchildren make it our duty to inform them of it. We usually let them in on our secret when they're around 14 or old enough to "get it." Why should they be tortured when we already have it figured out for them? If that's not familial love, I don't know what is.

Although our insanely happy grandmother, Lorraine, isn't a big drinker, there is no doubt she is the root of the zaniness in our family. Gram is an 88-year-old, tap-dance-teaching, swing-riding, sled-riding, boogie-boarding, parasailing, two-mile-a-day-walking, church-cleaning, lady-sitting (a nice way to say she "babysits" for older ladies) former Rockette. She runs circles around people half her age. When something unfamiliar is thrown her way, I have never witnessed her blink an eye. She has rolled with every punch she's ever received, and she has done it with a constant smile on her face.

Being the wackiest person I know is no small task, especially considering the cast of characters in my life, but Lorraine takes the cake by a mile. Refusing to use navigation in her car, she

chooses instead to call ahead to the police department of whatever town she's heading to and ask the officers for directions.
When she gets close to her destination, she always seems to pick
the biggest, scariest-looking man walking on the sidewalk, pull
her car next to him on the side of the road, and ask him exactly
where she should be heading. Once, when I begged her not to
talk to any motorcycle gang members on her way to an event,
she just dismissed my concerns, saying, "You really are missing

*My Grandma Lorraine in one of her Rockette
costumes, before a show. Radio City Music Hall, 1950.*

out on meeting some nice folks when you use that MapQuest business. I always get lucky and meet some new friends!"

Grandma—or "G-money," as some of our relatives call her (for no reason except two of her grandsons thought it was funny to say to her one day, and it stuck)—is always ready to have fun. She is like a little kid. When it snows, she calls from house to house to see if any of her grandchildren want to go sledding with her. Telling her you don't want to play in the snow just leads her to mercilessly heckle you; you end up feeling so embarrassed that your elderly granny is more fun than you are that you give in. Gram is an ace at persuasion, and she usually wins in the end.

When we're at the beach, Grandma pulls the same stuff. She sweetly badgers anyone who wants to hang out safely on the sand under an umbrella, calling you a "stick in the mud" for not wanting to dodge the waves with her. To locate her when she's swimming in the ocean on her boogie board, we just listen for her trademark "Wheeeeee heee!" and her ridiculous laugh. Or, we can just wait for her to get washed ashore, swept up by the waves like a teeny beached whale. With her bathing suit half up her butt and her hair sticking straight up on her head, she will stand up, look at us, and say, "God, that water is beautiful today! You're missing out." Then, she will prance right back into the current that just spit her out.

The playground is where she really shines, though. She challenges my nephews, her great-grandchildren, to race her on the swings. As the kids pump their little legs as fast as they can, she taunts them to try to get their swings higher than hers. Everyone has a blast, and Gram cracks up just as much as the kids do. Thankfully, she has finally stopped jumping off of the swings (although it took her much longer than it should have to become scared of breaking a hip).

Having 40 people crammed into her small, split-level house has never made her flinch. On holidays, her home pulses so loudly with our family's roars that you can hear it and feel it from your car when you pull into the driveway. Even after she needed a minor same-day knee surgery, she called everyone to come over for pizza the day after she went under the knife. She never even used crutches post-surgery. In fact, she didn't seem like a recovering surgery patient at all. As she walked around, she looked only as if she had just had a pedicure and didn't want to smudge her toenails. It didn't matter that she had just had arthroscopic knee surgery and had her cartilage repaired—with more than 20 people walking in and out of her house all night, she barely even batted an eyelash.

Although her children and grandchildren are party animals and have very colorful language, my grandmother is somehow G-rated. I have never heard her say a curse word. She will only have one drink (usually a screwdriver), and that's all she needs. I doubt there have ever been any R-rated thoughts or events in her life (besides baby-making, and even that, I'm sure, was very PG-13). Most of the beings she has spawned—and the maniacs they have created, in turn—have filthy mouths that curse, chug alcohol, smoke, and tell dirty jokes. I swear, she must have some sort of filter in her brain that turns the "F" word into "fudge" or that somehow makes our drunken family standing around her not appear to be the wasted, blubbering messes we truly are. She sincerely cannot see it. I don't know if it's by choice or because she prays it away, but it's hilarious either way. Fewer things are funnier than watching her as she has a conversation with

Grandma age 87, doing her thing at the playground.

my uncle Bob; seemingly oblivious to his truck driver mouth, she just smiles and nods as if he didn't just say the word "motherfucker" 30 times.

I have countless favorite things about my grandmother, but one of our traditions I cherish most is going to her house for family dinners. She always makes dinner, followed by her special homemade dessert. Her dessert is her "specialty," and she is always so excited to make it for us. After filling us all up on chicken cutlets, mashed potatoes, salad, and whatever other grandmother-ish thing she decides to make for us, she announces that we have to sit tight while she gets our dessert ready.

We all know what is coming, and it makes us all snicker and convulse with laughter. After several minutes clearing the table and talking while waiting for Grandma's creation, we hear Grandma's big announcement that dessert is ready.

We sit back down and she marches out, holding two bowls at a time until she's given one to each of us. We all try to keep straight faces as we examine our dessert: two little scoops of vanilla ice cream with chocolate sprinkles, which have half a banana standing straight up between the scoops. On the tip of the banana, there's a dollop of whipped cream and some maple syrup.

Grandma is dead serious as she sets them down. In Gram's G-rated world, she doesn't see anything X-rated about these phallic-shaped treats. It never would cross her mind that she has just passed out 20 desserts that look like wieners. Meanwhile, the rest of us cannot believe she can make that many and not think for one second, "Hmm, that's weird. This looks like a man's private part." The woman had six children for Christ's sake, so she clearly knows what a penis looks like. Somehow, though, she just smiles cluelessly as she digs proudly into her famous banana dessert.

Once, one of my cousins told her the dessert looked pecker-ish, and she just said, "What? Now, who would ever think that! It's supposed to look like a candle! It's just a banana and ice cream! Now, eat up."

So, we all did. And we still do—to this day. None of us have ever mentioned it again since then; it's almost as if we all subconsciously agreed not to let Grandma's G-rated bubble ever burst. We just give each other side-glances and try not to lose it in front of her.

As one big disgusting family, we just sit quietly and deep-throat our dessert.

Jackie vs. the Giant

I am not fit.

I don't run. I don't lift weights. I am *not* a big exerciser. At all.

Sure, I've belonged to gyms before, but, when you hate cardio with a passion and you're practically in tears every time you drag yourself to the gym, I don't think it counts for much.

In turn, as you can imagine, I am out of shape. I am a little bit on the chubby side, and I have spent most of my life hating myself for it. After all this time, I finally have gotten to a place where I can just be okay with what I look like. Besides, I get it—you only get what you give. If there's one thing I've learned from having been on a diet since I was 10 years old, it's that I'm happier when I'm eating than *not* eating.

So, I stick to the things that make me happy, and I just do what I can manage. I eat healthy (for the most part). I go for casual walks. To keep moving, I try to chase as many little kids around as I can (just for the record, I'm not a creep—I only do this wih my *friends'* kids). Besides that, I have made a conscious decision to let myself be happy and not worry about being skinny. I know very well that I won't ever be a waif: I only have eyes for food, and people who dream about food 24 hours a day don't tend to be waifs.

As hard as I try to keep my brain free from negative thoughts about how fat my ass is or how quickly my gut is starting to form, there is something I haven't quite conquered: feeling intimidated by super fit people. It's not even because I'm jealous of them—I couldn't care less about looking the way they do. But, I can't help getting extremely self-conscious around them, almost as if I can feel them hating me in all of my out-of-shape glory. In my mind (thank you, warped psyche), I can hear them calling me a "fat shit"—along with plenty of other weight-related insults I just can't seem to drown out.

All of that being said, before my best friend, Steve Weatherford, retired, he was literally "the NFL's fittest man"—officially given that title by *Muscle & Fitness* magazine, and more or less recognized for it everywhere else in the industry. (Trust me, the irony of the fittest professional athlete with the Pop-Tart-loving best friend isn't lost on me.)

Thankfully, Steve has never made me feel anything but okay with who I am: Steve is the kind of person who thinks you should do what makes you happy in life. And, considering working out has *never* made me happy (it just makes me dry heave), I'm grateful he's never pressed the issue. I'm sure he wishes I would be more active, but it's not something he makes me feel bad about.

My friendship with Steve has definitely made me realize that not every health freak I meet is judging me. In fact, it's helped me see that most of them probably don't even notice what I look like—there's a good chance that they're too concerned with their own appearance to even bother looking at me anyway.

Because Steve is so muscle-conscious, he admires many bodybuilders who work hard for their physiques. A few years ago, Steve was excited to find out that he and a famous bodybuilder shared a mutual respect for one another. In fact, not only did this other guy revere Steve, he also wanted to come see Steve play football.

Once Steve learned that, he started completely fangirling over this large, fit stranger. I wouldn't say I was jealous that Steve was constantly talking about this guy, but there was one thing that *was* getting on my nerves: this guy's never-ending flurry of social media posts about his admiration for Steve. They had just met, so this guy's adoring comments seemed unnecessarily over-the-top. Maybe I was acting like an elementary schooler, but the situation was really annoying me. It was that classic scenario: where you have a million really great friends, but, the moment someone else calls *your* best friend *their* best friend, it makes you want to punch the imposter in the face.

That's exactly how I started to feel about this mammoth-sized person: he was straddling the line of acting too "best friend-ish." Although it was completely irrational, seeing as this guy had never met me, I was still convinced that he was trying to make Steve forget about his short, fat, unkempt—but let's not forget, hilarious—best friend. My jealousy got the best of me. I pictured the two of them skipping together into a fluorescent-lighting sunset, muscle-bound arm in muscle-bound arm, and heading straight to the squat rack. I felt like I couldn't compete with that. This monster was not only acting like he was the best thing that ever happened to Steve, but also that the sun, the moon, and all the planets revolved around his enormous body. Everyone either had to fall in line to join his universe or be left behind—and I was already getting left in the dust.

Without ever even having met him, I didn't like him. My only basis: my assumption that, as a person, he must be the opposite of me, inside and out. Usually, I give people the benefit of the doubt and pride myself on being open-minded, so this was out of character for me. I was only letting myself see what I perceived to be his fakeness, and I had no interest in taking the time to try to find a positive quality about him. I was being a brat, and I knew it. Jealousy was making me into a seething jerk, and, while I didn't like it, I couldn't seem to stop it.

This guy decided he was going to come to one of Steve's preseason games. I was less than thrilled to learn that he and his two guests were going to sit near Steve's wife, Laura; our friend Joanna; and me. Honestly, I felt as if I would be meeting my archenemy.

On the dreaded day, I was so worked up that I began giving myself an internal lecture about being a nicer, more open-minded person.

Maybe I'm wrong...

I'll probably eat crow when this man and I finally meet...

He will possibly be the nicest person I've ever met...

The internal monologue continued the whole time we walked into the stadium and to our seats.

As we sat there waiting for the game to start, I was unreasonably nervous. Suddenly, a giant shadow appeared over us to our left. As I gazed toward the aisle, a man who seemed as wide as a building was towering over everyone. By his side, he had a very large muscle-bound lady, and another woman who seemed like a normal person, with him.

The gargantuan came barreling through the row, pulling his dog on a leash behind him. Yes, that's right. A *dog*. In a stadium. My problem was not with the dog, which was actually very cute, but with the arrogant, inconsiderate attitude of the selfish person who dragged him there. It was late August, and the poor dog was clearly super hot—and overwhelmed in the deafeningly loud stadium. I felt sorry for him, but he lay there loyally under his owner's feet for the next few hours, miserably enduring the discomfort.

As the crew plopped down into their seats, they barely said "hi" to Laura. Unsurprisingly, they completely disregarded Joanna and me.

I've been told I can't hide my feelings well. If I don't like you, you'll know it just by the look on my face. The second I saw this man and his posse, my earlier pep talk to myself became a distant memory. As much as I'd hate to admit I didn't like this man from first sight, that was pretty much the case. I could instantly tell he was not the type of person I would ever want to be friends with.

Everything he did proved me right.

A short while later, Joanna, Laura, and I got up to go to the bathroom. Apparently seeing an opportunity for us to do his bidding, he yelled to us, "I'll take a cold water."

Umm...last time I checked, we hadn't asked.

For Steve's sake, we attempted to put our irritation aside. Remaining civil, probably against our better judgment, we bought Muscle Man a bottle of water.

When we returned and handed the king his water, he was too busy eating to even say thank you. He wasn't eating stadium food. No, of course not. He was eating food he had brought *from home.* Let me rephrase that another way: he was eating *a Tupperware container full of steamed salmon and broccoli* that he had brought *from home.*

That was it for me. This person was completely in a world of his own, and I was not amused. When I encounter people with zero disregard for the folks around them or their well-being, it pisses me off. I am constantly very mindful of my surroundings and am tuned into how my presence affects the people around me. Maybe a little *too* hyperaware, but I don't care. I'd rather

The steamed salmon.

be too aware of myself than have my head up my asshole, apathetic to the effect my actions have on other people's happiness or unhappiness.

What kind of self-centered jerk would force the fans around him to inhale fishy salmon on a humid summer day? And what kind of heartless monster wouldn't even notice that his dog was dying of heat exhaustion less than a foot away from him? *This* guy. The guy who only cared if he—and he alone—was happy.

One glance at me, and my face undoubtedly said it all. But being the arrogant narcissist he seemed to be, I'm sure he didn't care for one second; in fact, he probably even relished in the fact I seemed intimidated by him.

I sat there stewing, ready to erupt at a moment's notice. I became obsessed with this block of a man sitting to my right. I couldn't stop staring at him and the aloof gang with him. I let their every move get on my nerves. He was on to his second round of steamed food before it was even halftime.

I couldn't believe the special treatment he expected—*and* got. It didn't matter that I was the (actual) best friend of one of the guys playing on the field; I still had to follow the rules every game, just like everyone else did. Hell, they barely let me bring a purse larger than an index card into the stadium. Meanwhile, somehow, not only was this beast able to bring his pet dog to a stadium where non–service animals weren't allowed, but there was also *plenty* of room for his suitcase-sized duffle bag. And no one had any objection to the fact he carried his own containers full of gourmet food, along with his own *metal* utensils, to a stadium that didn't allow outside food.

I guess that's the benefit of being so huge: no one will say no to anything you do, no matter how ridiculous it is. He probably could have walked in carrying a machete, saying he needed it to floss his teeth, and they would have said, "Ooooh, of course, obviously that's what it's for. Feel free to go right ahead in, Mr.

Bodybuilder. Disregard the metal detector alarm going off—that's only meant for people half your size. Just walk right in this way."

I let my disgust get the best of me, I guess. I kept peering over with an awful, seething look on my face. I was so shocked by his behavior that I could barely focus on anything else. Not to mention how completely bizarre it was that these two ladies with him seemed giddy with every move he made. With every absurdly self-centered thing he did, there was nothing but giggles and sounds of awe from his doting duo.

On my last irritated glance over in his direction, though, he caught my eye. I should have realized this would eventually happen. I don't know why I couldn't have just *stopped* looking over at him, as a normal adult would have done, but I couldn't. We then stared at each other for what felt like two full minutes. It seemed like a lifetime. I have no idea why, but I refused to look away.

Fuck him, I thought, *and his huge body, blown-out hair, fake tan, steamed salmon, and shirt that's too tight.* I was never going to let him win that staredown.

Finally, he interrupted our staring contest. From across the row, he said, "Do you want to fight me?"

I turned pale with fear and embarrassment. I have tough thoughts, but in real life I'm a five-foot-two wimp. Instantly losing the confidence my pent-up anger had given me, I stammered, "What?"

His girlfriend started giggling at me. She said, "Oh my God, babe, she is so nervous. Hahaha!"

This gave him more confidence. He sat up a little straighter in his seat, leaned his enormous body toward me, and said, "Do you"—pointing at me—"want to fight *me?*"—gesturing to his own huge chest.

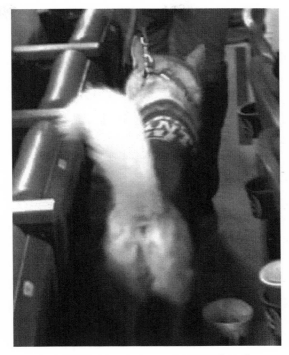

A (cute) dog wearing a sweater in MetLife stadium...
in August.

"What the fuck?" I muttered—mostly to myself, but still out loud. And then, with a final attempt at faux courage, I turned my head toward the field to watch my best friend play football. Half scared (and half trying not to laugh), I never looked back. I could hear them chortling next to me, but I didn't budge.

The monster squad decided to leave shortly after halftime, and I still didn't flinch. As they scooted by in their tight clothes, dragging their poor, helpless, heat-stricken dog behind them, I barely moved my eyeline away from the field in front of me. I refused to budge out of my seat, forcing them instead to clamber over me.

Just like that, Monster Man vanished—both from the game and from my life. Who would have won that epic fight, the world will never know.

(And, since I'm a total wuss, I am totally fine with not knowing.)

Call the Village

If you needed a remedy for your hangover and nausea, New Jersey Transit certainly would not be your first pick.

Nevertheless, there I sat at 8:00 a.m. on a warm Sunday morning in July, feeling miserable and foggy among a host of empty New Jersey Transit seats. After having partied all night with my friend Anthony, it was time for me to drag myself out of New York City. I was already feeling the effects of having bar-hopped until 3:00 a.m. (and having stuffed my face with greasy pizza before finally going to sleep). There was no way that a bumpy train ride, mixed with a hangover, was going to be pretty.

My head was pounding, my stomach felt queasy, and my mouth tasted as if I had licked cotton balls all night. Thinking that a little food and drink might help, I had bought a can of ginger ale and a bagel from inside New York Penn Station before I boarded the train. With a small nibble on the bagel, I quickly learned that the stale, gross, and moldy-tasting bagel wasn't going to help my situation at all. So, I resorted to slowly sipping my ginger ale as the train sluggishly started making its way back to New Jersey. I repeatedly swallowed hard, hoping I wouldn't spend the whole trip feeling sick to my stomach. As we rolled through the first two stops, I closed my eyes and told myself to take deep breaths.

In and out. In and out. In and out.

That helped me to feel slightly better, but I kept my eyes closed just in case.

In and out.

As I concentrated on my deep-breathing exercises, I heard someone loudly enter the car I was sitting in. Moments later, something rolled into my shoe, and my eyes instinctively popped open. I glanced down to see what had hit my foot: a few pieces of wadded-up notebook paper covered with doodles. I lifted my chin up, and, out of the corner of my eye, I saw a very large, very sweaty, wild-eyed man sitting across the aisle to my right. He was clutching a huge notebook that he was staring at intensely and scribbling onto. I realized he must have decided to discard some of his masterpieces by smashing them into a ball and chucking them my way.

It was purely instinct, but, at this point, shutting my eyes again suddenly felt like an unsafe thing to do.

This strange fellow was dressed like an adult-sized toddler. His huge size seemed oddly incompatible with his attire: a matching purple sweatsuit and white Velcro sneakers. He was drenched in perspiration, thanks to the July humidity and his rather warm outfit choice. He seemed extremely agitated, and he rocked his body back and forth continuously in his seat. From his appearance—and the fact he was mumbling loudly to himself—I surmised that he was either mentally ill or was on heavy-duty drugs.

The last thing I wanted to do was upset him—or draw attention to myself by acting nervous. So I tried instead to play it cool: I looked straight ahead and resumed my slow-breathing exercises. To help pass the time (and distract myself from the bizarreness happening next to me), I stared at my phone and scrolled mindlessly through pictures from the night before.

After a couple more stops passed by, this gigantic man suddenly stood up and started pacing furiously up and down the aisle. I subtly glanced up from my phone as my thoughts began running wild. I imagined my ugly driver's license picture displayed on the 6:00 p.m. news, as reporters sadly explained that this poor New Jersey girl's night of partying and pizza-bingeing had tragically ended with her murder by a crazed lunatic on an empty train car.

My brain was spinning.

What the fuck is this guy doing? Where's the goddamn conductor? Please walk into our car, Mr. Conductor! Pleasssse walk into our car! Should I move my seat, or will that make him freak out and grab me?

As I was just about to make a run for it, he sat down a few rows behind me. We were now on the same side of the aisle. I could see in the window reflection that he was switching back and forth between looking outside through the window and staring at the back of my head. He was in constant motion: barely able to contain himself and struggling to sit still, he reminded me of a little kid who desperately needed to use the bathroom. While he popped up and down back there, I said the rosary in my head, prayed I wouldn't get murdered, and eagerly counted down the number of stops (four) before this anxiety-ridden, slow-motion train ride from hell would be over.

That's when I heard him yell right to me.

"Hey! You in the glasses!"

I sat still. Didn't move. Didn't breathe. Practically played dead. But, somehow, that just brought on more yelling.

"Hellooo?! You in the glasses! Listen to me! Contact the village and tell them the lights are out!"

I could see his reflection behind me in the window, but I still didn't make any sudden movements. At this point, he cupped both hands around his mouth and continued again, this time louder.

"YOU IN THE GLASSES! Can you hear me? CALL. THE. VILLAGE. AND. TELL. THEM. THE. LIGHTS. ARE. OUT."

He was barking at me as if I was crazy. And maybe I *was* crazy.

Because, in a matter of seconds, I made the insane decision to acknowledge him.

I lifted my head and turned in his direction. Careful not to make direct eye contact with him, I said only one word to him: "okay." Then, I turned back around, my heart pounding. Now that I had engaged him, I was terrified he was going to come sit with me—or worse, punch me, or stab me to death.

That's when things took a really bizarre turn.

He didn't sit with me. He didn't punch me. He didn't stab me to death. Instead, he started singing.

The lyrics were about us, and they went something like this:
Heyyy you! Hey you in the glassesss.
Call the village (yeah)! And tellll them that that that…
The lights are out (uh huh)!
She said okay.
She said okay.
She said okay.
Okay!

As his lovely serenade came to an end, so did the accompanying drumbeat he was playing on the seats in front of him. Meanwhile, my mental countdown continued. *One more station stop to go.*

Suddenly, he stood straight up again, and I was overcome by a new fear: *What if he is getting off at the same stop as me?*

I started panicking anew, my thoughts once again racing. *What am I going to do if I have to hide from him? Or worse, if the situation calls for it, how will I possibly be able to run away from him? I'm in rough shape…and still wearing my outfit from last night…this is SO not the recipe for a successful getaway.*

We pulled up to my station, and I shot up quickly, grabbing all my stuff. He rushed up behind me and said, "Don't forget what I told you!" At the same time, he pumped his fist, celebrating as though he had just won a championship little league baseball game. Then, he promptly flopped back down, seemingly overcome by sudden exhaustion.

I hurried off the train, and, as I stepped onto the platform, I glanced back over my shoulder. My purple-clad "friend" was looking out the window, wildly waving at me—just as a child, climbing on the bus on his first day of school, would give his mom one final wave goodbye.

At that point, all I could think to do was wave back. So I did.

I can't talk my thumbs is heavy

Tongue

This is the best I ever felt this constitution

Hahahaha whaaaaaa

Gus and I had a full blown human convo. Nutssssss

My Thumbs Is Heavy

"My thumbs is heavy."

Now, I've always considered my cousin Mary to be my smartest relative, but a text message like this can certainly make you have doubts.

"What?" I texted back to Mary.

I tried to imagine what she meant, but I came up short. Mary would never be caught dead using such poor grammar.

Must be autocorrect, I told myself.

"My thumbs is heavy and I went to the Emerald City last night," Mary replied.

Umm…so much for my autocorrect theory.

"Mary? What. The. Fuck. Are you talking about?!"

I started getting nervous, so I called her. No answer. I called her a few more times. Still no answer. I was about to call her fiancé and ask him if *he* knew what the hell was wrong with her, but Mary called me back before I could. She was crying and whispering in the strangest, most deranged way I have ever heard—certainly from her, anyway.

I could barely decipher what she was saying. From what I could put together, she was mumbling something about having eaten pot and not handled it well. (Oh, but she had to go—she needed to call me later *after* work, just "in case the Tin Man was listening in" now on her work phone.)

I hung up and immediately dialed Frank, her fiancé. He answered the phone chuckling, as if he already knew why I was calling him. Before I could even say hello, Frank said, "So you talked to Mary today, huh?"

I asked him what the hell was wrong with her and if he needed me to drive down to their house. He reassured me she was going to be fine. He told me he had driven her to work and would pick her up in a few hours.

"Wait for her to call you," Frank added. "She had a rough night, but it's a good story that will only be funny if you hear it directly from her."

He could tell I still wasn't convinced she was okay, so he assured me her workday was a light one; if she hadn't already been scheduled to leave early, she would have called out sick.

At around 1:00 p.m. Mary called from Frank's car. She still sounded freaked out. She spoke as if she were on the run from the cops in a weird, overdramatized, cheesy '80s action movie.

"I ate two pot brownies last night," she said in a hurried whisper.

Mary had never smoked pot or tried any other drug in her life. So, it was hard for me to understand why *now*, at the age of 27, she had decided to try marijuana for the first time—as an edible. (For those who don't know, an edible is when pot is cooked into something, such as a brownie, a cookie, or even gummy bears.) When you eat an edible, it sometimes feels like nothing is happening to you; then, suddenly, it hits you in a delayed manner—and when it does, it's usually like a ton of bricks.

Because Mary had never tried anything like that before, she didn't know what to expect. Her only frame of reference was having seen people get high in movies. So, Mary ate one brownie and waited for that warm, fuzzy feeling movie characters appeared to get when *they* had pot. It didn't happen. So, Mary thought it wasn't working and decided to eat another one. Thanks to that somewhat questionable judgment call, there we found ourselves, about 24 hours later, with Mary nearly on the edge of insanity.

Apparently it wasn't just mere curiosity that pushed Mary to overdo it on the edibles. Between Mary's intense master's program, her full-time job managing a fertility office, and her time spent planning her wedding, Mary's life had become a perfect storm of chaos and stress. She was clearly struggling to handle things, which led her to completely out-of-character, spur-of-the-moment decision to try drugs for the first time.

As Mary and her more drug-experienced friend each ate their first brownie, Frank had tried to warn Mary to tread lightly. She didn't listen. Instead, Mary told her friend, "Let's have another one." Her friend didn't realize Mary had never experimented with marijuana before in her life. (Her friend probably just thought, "Whoa, okay. It's only Thursday, but sure, let's get wild.") So, in went the second fateful brownie.

Frank was absolutely right—it was well worth the wait to hear Mary tell the rest of the story. Without having heard Mary's own words, I probably wouldn't have believed this was what had happened to her next:

"Jackie, I am serious. This is not a joke, so don't you dare laugh. I went to the Emerald City last night. Like where Dorothy went. I talked to everyone in the city—the Scarecrow, the fucking Tin Man, even goddamn flying monkeys! It was amazing at first as I walked around, taking it all in. But then it got dark out, and the city seemed decrepit. Just as I started to feel scared, out of nowhere, Gus [Mary's dog] came walking toward me on the yellow brick road. He opened his dog mouth and *spoke* to me—not barking, but actual human words. For at least forty-five minutes we conversed, and I was so upset. I told him, 'Gus, I've known you all this time, and you pick *now* to tell me you speak like a person? We could've been communicating like this for the last four years!'"

Mary said that, after she reprimanded Gus in Oz, Gus only said one thing back to her: "You're going to throw up!"

That's when Mary's eyes readjusted slightly, and she recognized she was no longer skipping through the Emerald City. Although she could still "hear the sounds of Oz" (For my own entertainment, I really should have prodded her to elaborate—was it the cackling of the Wicked Witch? The roar of the cyclone?), she now was sitting on her bathroom floor, hugging her toilet.

When sober, Mary hates even the *thought* of hurling. Even in her altered state, she knew what would be coming: full projectile spewing. Sure enough, her worst nightmare happened: Mary began throwing up and continued doing so for the next three hours.

Hilariously, Mary claims she wasn't alone as she puked. No, supposedly, Mary had company. Apparently, *the Tin Man was with her*. According to Mary, he whispered "mean things" in her ear the entire time. In a string of insults, the Tin Man told Mary she hadn't belonged in the Emerald City anyway—and that she was getting what she deserved for having tried drugs, like an idiot.

Her fiancé eventually guided her upstairs to bed, all the while listening to her continue to fight with the Tin Man. When she woke up, she still felt terrible—and looked terrible; thanks to all of the violent puking, she had broken all the blood vessels in her eyes. But she knew that, no matter how awful she looked and felt, she still needed to go to work to tie up a few loose ends before the weekend.

Frank knew she shouldn't drive and called ahead to one of her coworkers. (Frank of course opted for the "didn't feel well all night" route, rather than the "had a horrible time handling her first high" one.) Frank asked her colleague to make sure Mary took it easy that day.

Mary's day at work wasn't exactly easy, but it was certainly unprecedented: never before had she walked into her office, left the lights off, locked the door behind her, and then spent the morning sitting on the carpet underneath her desk, compulsively rocking back and forth. Apparently, coworkers and clients tried repeatedly to get her attention, knocking on her door for 10 full minutes. Mary never heard the knocking.

Somewhat surprisingly, Mary did, at one point, hear her email alert go off. She slowly managed to pull herself up to check the computer above her. The message was from one of her patients ("Hi, Mary. Are you okay?"). Paranoid, Mary started panicking that this person not only knew that she had tried drugs but also that she was still high.

Trying to sound as casual as possible, Mary wrote back,

"Yup, never been better! Why do you ask?"

The patient's response was something like this: Because I have been banging on the door for the last 10 minutes, and I can see you through the window, seated on the floor, swaying. Can you please unlock the door now?

How do you even respond to something so embarrassing?

Well, if you're Mary, apparently what you do next is text your cousin, telling her, "My thumbs is heavy."

Polar Plunge

Every February since 2013, my friends and I have participated in a polar bear plunge in support of Special Olympics New Jersey. Usually held for charity, a polar bear plunge is an event at which people (sometimes thousands of them!) jump into a freezing cold body of water in the winter.

It may sound awful, but it is truly the most fun day of the year. Although it makes you cringe just *thinking* about what you are going to do, you are surrounded by so many thousands of happy, silly, wild, and creatively dressed plungers that you can't help but be wildly cheerful and crazy yourself.

Our second winter doing the plunge, there were 12 of us on our team, which we called "The Wet Bandits" after the duo of robbers in the movie, *Home Alone*. That year, our teammate Louis got a party bus to drive us all down the Garden State Parkway to Seaside Heights, New Jersey, for the plunge. We stocked up the bus with tons of alcohol, snacks, and silly costumes and accessories, like fake mustaches, crazy hats, and whatever other nonsense we could find at Party City.

The morning of the plunge, it was 10 degrees out—the kind of day that hurts your face when you're outside for more than five minutes. All of us started to panic. The first year we had plunged, it had been a freak 50-degree February day. The sun had shined bright, almost as if it were a July afternoon. We had still been cold that year, but we knew we had been very lucky.

That next year, however, was the opposite—the weather couldn't have been *worse*. By the time we all got onto the beach to take our plunge, it had started to snow. The temperature hadn't gone up even one degree since we had woken up that morning.

Anticipating running into the 33-degree ocean in snowy 10-degree weather was equally as bad as actually doing it. Bracing ourselves, our team ran together as fast as we could toward the ocean. The first step we took into the water, it felt as if we were trying to walk with frozen cement blocks on our feet. As we learned the hard way that year, your feet are not only the first to feel the God-awful frigid sand and water, they're also the hardest things to warm up after the plunge.

We ended our misery as quickly as we could. Popping right back out of the water almost as soon as we had entered it, we hurried directly to the bar on the boardwalk next to the beach. Shivering, we pushed our way through the drunken crowd to a huge table we had reserved in the back. Out in the open, we started changing into warm, dry clothes as quickly as possible. I am usually very easily embarrassed but, after that cold ocean hit me, all bets were off. When you are that cold, you truly lose all sense of modesty. I put on very baggy sweats and slipped off my bathing suit underneath, as hundreds of people around me changed, too.

Once we had nestled into some cozy clothes, we all immediately started drinking. Heavily. It was the only thing we could think to do to warm ourselves. After about two hours holed up in the bar, we finally looked outside and realized it was still snowing like crazy. Everything was completely covered with a few inches of snow. Although we were all pretty tipsy at that point, we made one of our only smart group decisions of the day: to just get on our party bus and head home before the weather got worse.

The roads proved to be dangerously icy, and we realized it was going to take a lot longer than expected to get home. We also discovered we had run out of alcohol on the bus, so, keeping our priorities in order, we asked our driver to stop at the first liquor store we saw. We all came out of the store with our arms full of whatever we could carry: beer, vodka, tequila—anything we saw. After replenishing our supply, we continued driving home. Thanks to the icy roads and slow-moving traffic, our trip, which normally would have taken about an hour and 15 minutes, looked like it would take more than twice that amount of time.

At that point, I was already very, very drunk. I am usually just a casual beer drinker or wine sipper, but about once a year I'll go on a binge-drinking fest. Sometimes it's for a special event; other times, it's for no reason other than I let myself get wasted by mistake. Truly, I hardly ever drink more than that.

After many years of learning the hard way, I know that I should never drink hard alcohol under any circumstances, especially in the form of shots. Stupidly, though, I ignored that important rule after the plunge. Disregarding any hangover lessons I had learned, I drank vodka with club soda continuously all day, downing four shots in the process. Hours later, I was practically speaking another language.

When we were about halfway home, we all suddenly had to go to the bathroom very badly. We abruptly stopped belting out

Me, very drunk after the polar plunge.

the hits of Frankie Valli and the Four Seasons at the top of our lungs (and dancing like lunatics) so that we could focus instead on where to pull over the bus. There were mostly guys on the bus, so it would be an easy pit stop for them, but for the three girls it was going to be tricky. I gave it some thought and, in my drunken state, I came up with what I believed was a sensible solution, at least for me.

My brilliant (read: not-so-brilliant) idea: pull down my pants, hoist my ass onto the cold, filthy metal guardrail on the side of the road, and pee over the side of the rail.

I am not athletic on a normal day, so, after drinking for eight hours straight, I obviously had even fewer motor skills at my disposal. Somehow, though, I still thought it was a foolproof idea to hop up next to my friend Jionni on the guardrail and start peeing.

Less than a second after giving myself a subconscious pat on the back for my clever plan, I (somewhat predictably) fell flat on my back. I landed with a thud in the snow.

All eyes were suddenly on me. Not only were my friends from the bus watching, but everyone caught in the slow-moving traffic on the Garden State Parkway gawked and beeped as they passed me by. As I lay there, I didn't even realize my pants were down. I was just thinking, *Am I okay? Did I just break my back and this is what dying feels like?*

I was in this haze for a few minutes until I felt the snap of cold on my ass. I heard the sound of Jionni (who is like a brother to me, although maybe not in this particular moment) howling with laughter. I finally stumbled up and shook off the shock of what had just happened. Pretending that everyone hadn't just seen my butthole, I pulled up my pants and shuffled awkwardly back to the bus. As I slumped down in my seat, the only thing I could think to do was put on one of the fake mustaches we had brought on the bus. With all of the drunken strength I had left, I started to sing along to the Four Seasons.

When we finally got close to home, we made yet another terrible decision. We thought it would be a great idea to take the bus to a local bar. We all stumbled into Luigi's in East Hanover, New Jersey, and it was filled with tons of people we knew. They all looked at us in horror at the sight of our drunkenness and seemed particularly appalled by me, most likely because I was still sporting my pretend mustache.

We ordered more drinks that we didn't need and tried to carry on normal conversations with these people. They weren't nearly as drunk as we were, so, needless to say, the conversation wasn't exactly scintillating. The rest of the night was such a blur that I had to try the next day to piece it together through pictures, videos, and text messages.

Despite drinking all day and night, I eventually somehow got back to my house and stumbled into my bed. What seemed like only a minute later, I was woken up by the sound of my iPad ringing. (Honestly, I didn't even know an iPad could ring.) My phone was dead, and I had completely disregarded the fact that I had a flight to Florida scheduled for the day after the plunge. Not to mention I had a 5:00 a.m. car service scheduled to pick me up. While I had been getting wasted the day before, I had forgotten to set an alarm for myself.

I tried to understand what the person talking out of my iPad was saying. I eventually put it all together: I realized it was a woman from the car service company on the phone. She informed me that, due to the snow, my driver was going to be late. She also said I had to share the ride with another two people because their drivers didn't report to work in the bad weather.

I jumped up, still in my outfit and fake mustache from the night before. I became frustrated when I couldn't find any of my luggage, only to realize that was because I hadn't actually packed anything yet for my trip. I was so pissed at myself, and I was also embarrassed that I stunk like alcohol. I quickly grabbed whatever I thought I would need, threw everything into my carry-on bag, and jumped into the shower. Meanwhile, the post-hangover nausea set in.

Just as I was getting dressed, the driver pulled up. I got

into the minivan, joining two other (very chatty) women who were also on their way to Newark Airport and headed to Fort Myers, Florida, as well. As the ladies began talking my ear off, I put on my winter hat over my soaking wet hair and started concentrating on not puking. I tried to be as polite as I could possibly manage, despite how I was feeling: I answered many of their questions and made minimal small talk. By the time we were halfway to the airport, though, I couldn't take it anymore. I pulled my knit hat down as far as it would go and wrapped my scarf around my face so they would hopefully stop talking to me and get the hint that I was not feeling well.

We pulled up to the United Airlines terminal, and I darted over to the first garbage can I saw. I didn't actually make it. I barfed my guts out all over the side of the can and onto my huge scarf. I stood frozen for a minute, not sure what to do, as people walked by gagging and looking repulsed by me. I finally pulled myself together and took my scarf off, throwing it into the trash. I went through security and headed right for an airport convenience store, where I bought a toothbrush, toothpaste, and some Advil. I tried to get my shit together quickly in the bathroom before I finally boarded the plane.

At that point, I pretty much just wanted to die—like actually go straight to the pearly gates—instead of feel as awful as I did from my hangover and from that morning's embarrassment. I'm a horrendous flyer normally, but this time was even worse: I felt like a delinquent for just having vomited in front of half the people I now had to share an airplane with. I began praying that I wouldn't have to throw up again and, of course, that the plane wouldn't crash. (I certainly didn't want these people's last thoughts before they died to be about how disgusting I am.)

When we landed three hours later in Fort Myers, my father, who was waiting right outside of the gate, saw me walking toward him. At first, he looked so excited to see his only daughter strolling up the hallway, but, as I got closer, I could see his face change.

The first words he spoke to me after not having seen me in two months: "Jesus Christ! What the hell happened to you?"

My father's words must have triggered something in my mind because, all at once, my memory of the entire night before finally came back to me. It hit me like a ton of bricks in the head. I was horrified when I suddenly remembered something about the night before—something I had forgotten: I had flashed my bare asshole for the world to see.

Thanks to a guardrail, an excess of alcohol, and my bare butthole, the Wet Bandits—and our yearly polar plunge—will never be the same.

Pants On, Pants Off

This is a strange thing to admit, but, by the time I was 35, I had never had a massage. That's not to say I didn't want one or need one. My back and shoulders were always sore from long hours of standing and styling hair, so the occasional (or regular) massage probably would have done wonders. But, I just never could work up the nerve to schedule one.

Unfortunately, being exceptionally self-conscious often gets in my way—and my irrational fear of massages was case in point. I chronically avoided getting one, worried I'd spend the whole time panicking that my butt was hanging out of the sheets or that the massage therapist was judging my back fat. I wanted so badly to be one of those people who could strip their clothes off, lie down, and let a complete stranger rub their back without a care in the world. But that carefree self-confidence just wasn't in my nature, and I knew it never would be.

The year I was 35 was the same year my youngest cousin, Livi, turned 15 (her birthday is on January 8). She is the kind of kid who has everything anyone would ever want or need. So on her birthday that year, instead of buying her a present she didn't need, like I do every year, I asked her if she wanted to celebrate her birthday a different way: by doing something fun together.

She thought about it for a few minutes before she decisively made up her mind: we were going to get massages together.

Gulp. *Just kidding, Livi! I take it back!*

I really wished I had seen that one coming.

"Okay, great," I said, feigning cheerfulness. I already regretted that I didn't just buy her another stupid fucking purse, like I had last year.

We were trying to get massages later that day, but, because it was a Sunday, I figured it wouldn't be easy to find an open spa. I began calling around trying to find a place that had two available appointments at the same time on such short notice. I prayed there wouldn't be any place that could accommodate us, but my prayers went unanswered. The third place I called had two operators available (*Thanks a lot, "Maria and Mike"!*) at the same time. As a protective older cousin, I wasn't going to let my 15-year-old cousin go to a man, so I told the woman on the phone that I would go to Mike and Livi would go to Maria.

As a painfully self-conscious human and a massage newbie, I was facing one of my fears head-on. Not only was I getting my first massage ever, but now I had to go to a *man*—a man who would undoubtedly think I was disgusting and fat.

Livi got into my car an hour later, and we started driving to the spa. I spent the car ride picturing Mike as this hot, six-foot-tall man who would dry heave the moment he saw me. Livi had no clue how nervous I was, and, even though I felt like an immature asshole, I tried my best to give off an adult vibe. We walked in and started filling out the usual paperwork.

ANY ALLERGIES? "Yes, to the hands of judgmental handsome men," I wanted to write. I knew it was only a matter of seconds before that judgmental handsome man would strut out and cringe at the sight of his grotesque next client. Maria came out first to get Livi, and Livi went skipping gleefully into the hallway, not worrying about a thing.

My heart started pounding as I saw the doorknob turning. The door opened, and Mike was suddenly standing in front of me. Mike was the same height and size as me, which instantly made me feel less intimidated. He was handsome, looked to be about my father's age, and (eventually) told me he was Egyptian. Hearing his adorable accent made me unexpectedly relieved, and I felt relatively calm as he led me into the room. He asked to see my hands, and he looked them over with a serious face. As he squeezed a couple of my fingers and pressed his fingers into my palm, I assumed he was trying to tell if I was dehydrated. He then told me to undress to my comfort level and get under the blankets facedown. He exited the room and closed the door behind him.

Left alone without the adorable man (and his endearing accent) to keep me calm, I started freaking out again. *Do I take my pants off or not?* Never having had a massage before, I didn't know what was right. I texted a few friends and, *of course*, no one got back to me quickly enough. As usually happens in these types of situations, I started having a typical Jackie inner debate with myself.

Finally, I decided that leaving them on and having Mike *ask* me to remove them was way less embarrassing than the alternative: taking them off and having Mike tell me to put them back on because my striptease act was inappropriate. So I lay down, naked from the waist up (but still sporting my baggy sweatpants), and waited for him to come back in.

When Mike eventually returned, he started asking me questions about what I did for a living and what preference I had (if any) for the amount of pressure he used during his massage. We made small talk, which made me feel more at ease. He informed me that his children had wanted to come to the US to go to college and live here after they graduated, so he and his wife followed them here from Egypt. Mike told me that he had actually been a general surgeon in his country, but the cost to get his license in America was very high and he had since come to enjoy being a masseur. Not only was he was making good money as a masseur, but he felt like he was still helping people and making a difference in their health in a different way: through massage.

He seemed to be able to figure out almost everything about me instinctively. He could tell I got very bad migraines and tended to lean on my right leg while standing all day at work. Mike had actually been reading my palms earlier. From what he saw on my hands, I seemed to be a very nice person, but I was doing too many things for other people. His conclusion: helping others without being thanked was making me repress my anger.

"Stop that!" he said. "You're making yourself sick! Only do what you can without putting yourself second constantly. You have to do things for yourself, too."

Sheesh, Mike! Look right into my soul why don't you!

I didn't get a chance to say that (or anything else) out loud, as the conversation abruptly turned.

"What is *this*?!" Mike exclaimed. "Why have you left your pants on?"

He had just moved to the other end of the table to massage my feet—only then had he spotted my pants. I reminded him that he had told me to undress to my comfort level. *This* was my comfort level.

"I meant whether you would leave your underwear on or not," he said, half laughing.

I started to giggle, embarrassed. He turned around so I could take them off. At that point, though, I was completely blind without my glasses on, so I had no idea if he was looking my way or not. The only thing I did know was that showing my boobs to Mike from Egypt was definitely not on my to-do list for the day.

While lying flat on my stomach, I started shimmying off my pants as best I could. Practically all of my worst fears about getting massaged (*and* embarrassing myself while getting massaged) were coming true. It made me feel a little nauseous.

I broke out into a full-blown sweat at the thought of the crappy blankets falling off and Mike seeing me in my birthday-suit glory. My vivid imagination kept going: *What if I fall off the table altogether?*

Miraculously, I got the pants far enough past my butt that I could use my feet to help strip them off of my legs the rest of the way. I hooked my big toe around the waistband of my pants and scooted off one pant leg, then the other. It was the world's least graceful act of pants-removal ever. As I reached down to grab the pants, flailing around on the table and making lots of unintended noises, I could hear Mike belly-laughing at my distress. Undeterred, I blindly chucked them across the room. They hit the wall with a soft thud and slid down to the floor.

When Mike asked if the coast was clear, I could tell he was still chuckling at my mistake. He proceeded to tell me several more times that he couldn't believe I had never had a massage and didn't know I was supposed to take my pants off.

Okay, Mike. Let it go. Just focus on rubbing my fat feet.

The hour passed much more quickly than I ever would have expected. Mike left so I could get dressed. I walked across the room, picked up my pants, and slipped them on. As I exited the room to get Livi and pay our bill, Mike stood in the hallway, still grinning from ear to ear and shaking his head in disbelief. He told me I made his day by leaving my pants on; in fact, he couldn't wait to go home and tell his wife about my massage.

Oh, great. I'm so glad.

Thanks to Mike, I began to think that maybe—just maybe— massages aren't so horrible.

That was, of course, before I had my *second* massage.

Prior to that second fateful massage, my lower back had been killing me for about two weeks. As usual, I was wishing it away, unwilling to go to the doctor like a normal adult would. I wore sensible shoes while I stood at work every day; used a heating pad, ice packs, Icy Hot rub, and Advil; and tried any other home remedy I could think of. Nothing worked. That weekend was crazy busy at work and, by the time I got home that Saturday night, I was in agony. I shuffled up the stairs into my house, took a huge dose of whatever anti-inflammatory I could find fastest, and went to bed. On Sunday, I woke up determined to feel better. Since I couldn't get in contact with my chiropractor until Monday, I started calling everyone I know asking for any advice to help with my back pain. One of my coworkers suggested a local massage parlor that she had been to.

"It's a walk-in place that has good prices," she said.

After the humiliating incident during my first massage, I was nervous about making a jerk of myself again, but the pain made me willing to try anything.

I pulled up to the massage parlor and instantly felt as if I were making a mistake. The sign out front had missing letters; in the window was a huge, shiny plastic Buddha statue with a crack down the middle. I approached the front desk and told the woman there I needed a half-hour massage. She walked me over to a "room" in the back corner ("room" is a bit of a stretch, as there were no walls—just curtains and a flimsy wooden door that had somehow been configured to hang loosely off of the curtains).

Another woman came in behind me, motioned with her hands for me to remove my clothes, and said the words "take off." After she exited the "room," I realized there was only a sheet to cover the massage bed and nothing for me to cover myself with. Not knowing what to do, I just stood there like a dummy.

She came back a few minutes later and was visibly annoyed that I still had my clothes on.

"Take off!" she hollered at me, still miming with her hands. "Take off clothes!"

"There. Is. No. Blanket. To. Cover. Myself. With!" I said loudly in exasperation.

She only said one word ("Oh") before she walked out. Back in an instant, she handed me a beach towel.

"This," she said curtly. She walked out again.

I have no idea why I didn't just leave at that point. It was uncomfortable to strip down in a fake room (with a door that couldn't even shut) and to cover myself with nothing more than a beach towel. I guess I figured, "What the hell? I'm already here." So I eventually took my clothes off, lay down, and covered my fat body with the skimpy beach towel. The same woman returned—still irritated with me, but clearly relieved I was finally naked.

She began pushing on my lower back through the towel, going back and forth—side to side—from one hip to the other. I tried not to yelp from the pain.

This lady must know what she's doing, if she can tell my lower back hurts without even asking me any questions.

I hoped I was right.

The table was almost as wide as a bed, so she hopped up on the table, putting her knees by my torso. As she leaned over me, her feet were close to where my face was (you know, in the little face-hole thing). Like I've said, I am inexperienced in the massage department, so I honestly had no clue if what she was doing was normal or not.

Just stop being uptight and overthinking this; she's going to make you feel better.

Suddenly, without any warning, she ripped my underpants off. I don't mean she gently lowered them. I mean she *tugged* on them, swiftly pulling them down to my knees.

What the fuck?!

She proceeded to rub my bare butt cheeks for close to 10 minutes. I began panicking but said nothing. As an awkward person, I don't deal with things like that well. I could have acted like a grown-up and said, "I'm not comfortable with this." But I didn't. Instead, I started to laugh uncontrollably until I began to cry. Tears and snot poured from my face, cascading through the face-hole and onto the floor below me.

The masseuse asked a few times, "You okay?" She must have thought I was crying from pain (or maybe even sadness). It didn't, however, stop her from continuing to massage my butt cheeks in a rough circular motion the entire time.

I am modest and have never been anything close to an

exhibitionist in my entire life, so the fact that my bare butt was out in the open was pretty much my worst nightmare. That is, until I realized that this stranger not only was rubbing my butt but, with her vigorous circular motion, was probably also able to see my (gulp) asshole in all its glory. This was essentially the worst of any worst-case massage scenario I could have ever imagined.

She eventually stopped tenderizing my cutlets of pure fat, pulled my underpants up, and covered me back up with the beach towel. I've never appreciated a beach towel more than I did at that moment. I prayed the whole ordeal was now over.

It wasn't.

Next, the woman stood up on the table. Holding onto a bar above her head, she proceeded to traipse up and down my back—using her toes as leverage—and then squeezing whatever she could around my spine, too. After tap-dancing her little heart out (a.k.a. steamrolling up and down my body), she jumped down and finished up the remaining minutes of my massage by beating the shit out of whatever else was left on my body that she hadn't touched yet. The awful massage *finally* ended, and she charged out of the "room." I stood up and put my clothes back on as quickly as I could.

I looked around the room and took in where I was. After I glanced again at the flimsy sheet on the bed, the huge tub of Vaseline, a clear ketchup-like bottle of something that looked like cooking oil, and the bar across the ceiling, it finally clicked: *Maybe I am at a pervert place.* Still in as much pain as (if not more than) I had been when I first walked in, I hobbled up to the front desk. I paid—and then dragged my aching body out of the building—as fast as I could.

Back in the safety of my car, I sat and laughed for quite a while. I could barely process everything that had just happened.

Was that a "true" massage experience? Or had I just been assaulted?

I couldn't believe that was something people actually *paid* for, but what did I know? Maybe it was, maybe it wasn't, but I knew one thing for sure: there wouldn't be a third foray into the massage world for me.

My massage-getting career, short-lived as it was, was officially over. From now on, there would be nothing but purses for Livi. And beach towels would cover my bathing, not birthday, suit.

Eyebrow Stains

I always wanted to be a hairstylist. From the time I was four years old, I would put perm rollers into my dolls' hair, wet their hair in the sink, and then take the rollers out the next morning. Not only did I want my dolls to have curly hair like I did, I also wanted to be the one who gave it to them.

Not one single person in my life was surprised that I went to beauty school. Seventeen years later, no one was shocked either by the fact I still worked at the same salon, which was owned by one of my best friends. The reason to become a stylist is because you love doing hair, but the reason to *stay* working as a hairstylist for as long as I have is because of the wonderful clients. They truly turn into your family. I have been through so much with my clients over the years: births, deaths, marriages, operations, illnesses, and countless other life events—both big and small. I wouldn't change any of those experiences; they've helped define our relationships and allowed us to grow close over the years.

I appreciate all of my clients, old and new. One day, I was thrilled to learn that a new client on my schedule was actually the grandmother of one of my other clients. Since I adored my client, and I knew she loved her grandmother very much, I was excited to finally get to meet her grandmother, Mildred.

On the day of her appointment, Mildred shuffled in. She sported a big puffy blonde hairdo, a fur coat, and huge, expensive sunglasses, yet she carried a paper Macy's shopping bag as her purse. She walked very slowly, with the help of a cane with a bedazzled handle. Mildred may have lacked the ability to walk well or see much at all, but she made up for it by being sharp as a tack. With her smart-ass mouth, she made me laugh within the first five minutes she was in my seat.

After our initial small talk about what to do with her hair, I started to brush the dye onto her gray roots. She told me to make sure I put lots of dye on her eyebrows, too, so I complied. We became fast friends. I enjoyed talking to Mildred so much that we sat down to drink coffee and chitchat for a few minutes after I was done applying her color. Once my next client came in, I left Mildred alone for a short time in order to put color on the other client's hair.

When I walked by Mildred a short while after, she called to me, "Honey, I have to piddle!" Assuming she could go alone and forgetting that she wasn't stable on her feet, I just said "okay" and kept walking.

A little bit later, I passed her again. She yelled once more, this time louder.

"Honey, you have to take me. I can't see where I'm going! It's an emergency!"

A feeling of dread overwhelmed me. Sure, she was one of the coolest old ladies I had ever met. And sure, from the minute I had met her, it had felt as if we were old friends. But, I usually don't bring my old friends to take a pee.

I looked around the salon, hoping to catch someone else's

eye and beg that other person to help Mildred so I wouldn't have to. No one met my gaze, and I knew helping her would be my responsibility—and mine alone—since her family had dropped her off.

Facing the inevitable, I swooped my arm under hers to help her up. As I guided her to the bathroom, I prayed silently that I wouldn't have to wipe her ass and that she wouldn't be wearing a diaper. Seeing her crawl toward the restroom at a snail's pace only worsened my fears: all I could do was hope we made it before she had an accident in her pants and on our floor.

Please, God, if you hear me, I'm sorry for any terrible thing I've ever done in my whole life. Please, please, please don't let this happen. I promise to be a better person. I promise to go to church more. But, God, I really, REALLY can't wipe the ass of an adult I'm not related to. Please, God, I love you. Amen. (made sign of the cross)

We finally reached the bathroom at the back of the salon. She went inside, shut the door, and yelled loudly, "Honey, don't go anywhere! I'm going to need you in a minute."

Fuck.

At that point, I pleaded desperately with God. I practically *begged*. I said anything—and everything—that came to mind.

I'll work out more. I'm sorry about cheating on all those tests in high school. I promise to do more charity work and feed the homeless. That one time when I stole that candleholder on the boardwalk, I feel terrible about that—but I was a kid, and peer pressure got me! I promise to say three hundred Our Fathers and four hundred Hail Marys if you can help me not have to see anything disgusting.

I continued to pray, standing outside the door and listening carefully to make sure Mildred didn't fall. After a few minutes, I heard her bellow, "I'm ready for you!"

I took a deep breath and opened the door. I was afraid of what I'd see. When I slowly opened my eyes, Mildred was standing up, smiling at me.

"You have to pull up my underwear and pants," she said. "I have arthritis."

For a fleeting moment, I was happy that I didn't have to wipe her behind. That feeling didn't last long, though, once I realized I would have to see her bare 95-year-old ass.

Just do it, Jackie, I told myself. *Do it quickly.*

Standing behind Mildred, I grabbed her underwear and pants at the same time with both hands. I pulled up as swiftly and as hard as I could, hoping that, if the first tug was successful, I wouldn't need to go back in for a second.

Only after I heard a loud thud did I realize Mildred hadn't been holding onto her cane. Thanks to my obliviousness, and the force of my tug, she had slammed her face into the wall. *Hard.*

I held my breath. I wasn't sure what to do. After a few moments, Mildred laughed nervously, and relief swept over me. I laughed, too, and asked if she was okay.

"I'm fine, dear," she said.

As she peeled her face from the wall, I saw the distinct outline of her hairline and her two eyebrows on the wall. Dye from her hair and eyebrows had left behind a Mildred-shaped imprint.

I handed Mildred's cane to her, and we shuffled to the front of the salon. Despite Mildred's constant reassurances she was fine, I continued to quiz her to make sure she actually was okay. As I cut and styled her hair, I studied her the entire time, looking for signs of a black eye or a bloody nose. She seemed to still have her wits about her. That gave me relief, as I was worried she might have gotten a concussion.

When Mildred's daughter returned, I briefly described what had happened. Her daughter seemed concerned I had smashed her face, of course. But, after her daughter examined her for bruises and Mildred said she was fine, her daughter told me not to feel bad, especially because she was unharmed. Mildred's daughter also wished she had warned me that Mildred was supposed to avoid coffee for health reasons. (Yep, that would have been helpful.)

Once they left, I returned to the bathroom and tried scrubbing the color off of the wall before it permanently stained. It was too late.

The outline of Mildred's hair and eyebrows remained stained on our wall for months, no matter how hard we tried to scrub it clean. It eventually faded away—for the most part. Today, if you look hard enough, you can actually still see the faint outline of her face staring back at you while you use the toilet.

Like Big Brother, Mildred is always watching you.

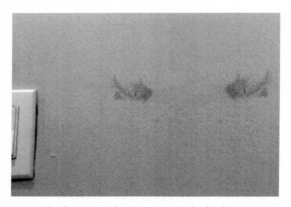

The famous eyebrow stains on the bathroom wall of The salon where I work

Bury Christmas

For many people, Christmastime can be the best part of the year—a time filled with family, love, togetherness, and Christmas spirit. I feel that way for the most part, but the magic often gets lost when your house is full of guests overstaying their welcome.

It was December 2005. I was 25 years old, and I had lived in my condo for almost a year at that point. While my condo may not have been much to look at, it was mine, and I was happy to finally have a place of my own.

My dad and Lynn had been living half the year in New Jersey ("down the shore") and the other half in Fort Myers, Florida. For the holidays that year, they planned to leave two days after Christmas to drive down south and throw a New Year's Eve party in Fort Myers; until then, they were staying with me for the holidays. As if that weren't chaotic enough, Lynn had also brought along her two dogs, with whom she had a *very* obsessive relationship. (Obsessive as in she would dress them up in weird outfits, kiss them right on their lips any chance she could, only serve them food on actual dinner plates so they felt like part of the family, apply makeup on their hairy faces every morning after she put on her own makeup, and speak to those dogs more than she spoke to anyone in our family, including my dad.)

From the moment my stepmother arrived, she began popping pills and drinking Pinot Grigio, as always. As Lynn stumbled aimlessly from room to room, her two dogs followed her around like shadows. Watching them trace her zigzagged path was every bit as comical as it sounds.

Coconut, Lynn's bichon frise, and I hated each other. He was an asshole. A white, fluffy nightmare. He pissed everywhere and chewed anything in sight. Shoes, purses, socks—it didn't matter. It was as if he tried his hardest to make me want to kill him.

Lynn's other dog, Francesca, was a pretty, sweet, medium-sized black and brown mutt. The complete opposite of Coconut, Francesca not only was happy, but also *loved* everyone she met. The poor thing had been behaving funny since she had come up north; she was acting lethargic and out of sorts, and she had thrown up a couple of times. Panicked about it, my dad checked on her constantly.

(Meanwhile, while poor Francesca suffered, Coconut bit my dog, Lucy—if there was one thing Coconut was good at, it was making me despise him more and more every minute we were together.)

When it was time to leave the house to celebrate Christmas Eve dinner with our extended family, Francesca seemed to be doing a little better, so we decided it was safe to leave her for the night. We spent most of Christmas Eve at my uncle's house in Denville, New Jersey. By the time we came home, Lynn, who had sucked down an assortment of drinks, was barely able to walk up the stairs on her own. She was stumbling around and slurring when we walked in to find a big pile of dog barf in the living room. Figuring it was Francesca who had made the mess, Lynn said it would help the dog's upset stomach if she gave Francesca a Zantac antacid pill. Without even thinking twice, Lynn wrapped up a pill in a piece of cheese and fed it to her sick dog.

I may not be a veterinarian, and I may not be the smartest person in the world, but I definitely had a feeling that wasn't the best idea. At my wit's end from dealing with drunk Lynn and cleaning up dog barf, I decided to just go to bed and hide from all of the dysfunction.

I woke up at 5:30 a.m. to a series of muffled sounds, including the sound of my own dog scratching at my bedroom door. Lucy was desperate to get out to see what all the commotion was, so I walked into the living room with her. We found Lynn crying on the floor. Francesca was next to her, breathing slowly and heavily.

As my dad paced around the kitchen, I slowly surmised what had happened. I'm fairly certain that in Lynn's foggy state—and with her wide array of pills to choose from—Lynn got confused, grabbed the wrong one, and gave Francesca one of her Xanax anxiety pills by mistake.

Sadly, poor Francesca took her last breath while my dad, Lynn, Lucy, Coconut, and I watched in stunned silence. I had never seen anyone or anything take its last breath before. It was awful, sobering, and alarming watching her suffer during those last few breaths, while we sat there helplessly. Francesca had been a good dog, and I was genuinely sad to see her go.

As soon as Francesca passed, Lynn erupted in screams, and my dad began punching the wall. Trying to keep a level head, I wondered practically what we could even do at that point. It was not even 6:00 a.m. on Christmas morning, so the vet obviously wasn't answering his phone. It was about 20 degrees out, and it had been equally as cold for the two weeks before that, so we knew the ground would be hard as a rock if we attempted to bury her.

I left the room and called my brother. Neil and his wife, Jen, had just moved into their new house a few months before. It was their first Christmas in the house together. Neil answered, annoyed and ready to kick my ass for waking him up so early. I tried to quickly relay what had happened, but my dad grabbed the phone.

"Neil, we're burying Francesca in your backyard," my dad said. "Call Sal and ask him if he can help us."

I took the phone back, and I could sense my brother's anxiety and discomfort with the situation. I knew he didn't want to have to wake up his sleeping father-in-law, Sal, that early. And he *especially* didn't want to awaken Jen: the last thing he wanted to tell her was that they would spend their first Christmas morning in their new home burying a dead dog in their yard at 6:00 a.m.

Being the dependable big brother he is, and knowing how stressed out we all were at my house, Neil showed up at my doorstep in less than 10 minutes. His father-in-law was by his side. Poor Sal. I'm sure he would have rather been sleeping, but he must have known my brother was really desperate to have woken him up before the sun came up on Christmas morning.

As my father cried inconsolably in the kitchen, my brother and I awkwardly glanced at each other. Without having to speak, we both knew we were thinking the same thing: that this was our weirdest Christmas ever. We had had some really strange ones over the years, but this was in a league of its own.

It suddenly dawned on me that, since it was Christmas, we were all supposed to give each other presents soon. All I could selfishly think of was, *How the hell am I supposed to give my dad his new iPod and Yankees shirt now?* And also, *Why couldn't it have been frigging Coconut that croaked?* Hating myself for having those thoughts, particularly the second one, I tried to push them out of my head.

We all stood around for a few minutes until my dad collected himself abruptly and said, "Okay, let's get this over with." He grabbed every old blanket and towel he could find and laid them on the floor next to the dog's body. He looked over at us and said, "Don't watch—it's going to be disgusting."

I heard him, but I couldn't take my eyes off of Francesca as he lifted her up. She was as stiff as a board. I had never seen anything like it. She was stretched out just like a dead dog would have looked in a cartoon. My dad, my brother, and Sal wrapped up her frozen body and put her in the back of my brother's car. My brother has pretty severe aversions to anything or anyone that's sick, let alone *dead*, so having an animal's corpse in his trunk was pretty much his worst nightmare.

As they brought Francesca to his backyard to bury her, my brother started panicking about how they would dig a hole in the frozen dirt deep enough to bury Francesca. My father, my brother, and Sal began digging with all of their strength, while also trying to avoid making too much noise: the last thing we wanted to do was wake up the neighbors at such an early hour. I'm sure if any of the neighbors had seen what was going on, they definitely would have been alarmed. Nothing says "call the cops" like a group of people— with *shovels*—huddled before dawn around a concealed object. I mean, we had already been asking ourselves how much more ridiculous that DellaTorre holiday could get, and that was before we had been dragging a wrapped-up dog corpse through the yard.

After about an hour and a half, the guys were able to dig a hole that was deep enough to fit Francesca's body. It was probably not as deep as it should have been, but the large lump in my brother's yard was par for the course that day. With that, we laid poor Francesca to rest.

After the deed was done, my dad came back to my house and started drinking a gigantic glass full of scotch. I had never ever wanted to know that, when a living thing dies, it releases all of its bodily fluids; yet, here I was on Christmas morning, wanting to barf as I stared at the gross stain on my carpet where the dog had died and left us with her bodily fluids. With a cigarette hanging out of her mouth, Lynn sat on the floor, furiously scrubbing the stain. I don't think she knew what else to do with herself, other than try to wipe away the memory of the horrible day. She cleaned for hours, but the stain didn't go away. For years, no matter what I tried to use on it, it never budged. Until I replaced my carpet a couple of years later, everyone knew that spot as "the death stain." Even though I covered it with an area rug just days after the dog had died, we all still continued to step around that spot for years.

At that point, I had no idea how to spend the rest of my Christmas, but I knew I couldn't stand to be in the house with the death stain much longer. I showered in a vain attempt to wash the terrible day off of me, and then I fled to see my best friend, Faith. I rattled off the whole story from start to finish in what felt like one huge run-on sentence. Faith, her mom, and her sister did what they could to help me feel better and to turn my Christmas around, but, to this day, I still cannot hear anyone mention dead dogs, statues of dogs, iPods, Pinot Grigio, Zantac, or Xanax without being reminded of that awful, bizarre day.

At least I have it better than my brother, though: every heavy rain reminds him that Francesca is buried shallowly in his yard, and he watches from the window, wondering if she will wash up one of these days.

Lynn and Francesca.

The most evil dog that ever lived, Coconut.

Acknowledgments

I want to thank my editor Alexandra for helping me through this three-year-long journey. I can't tell you how much I appreciate all of your hard work and patience with me.

To Charlie, for guiding me through this self-publishing process.

To Steve, for the constant daily pep talks, for pushing me through some pretty crappy days, and for your encouragement to get this book finally finished.

To Joanna, for your never-ending advice on appropriateness for this book (and in life). Thanks for always being a voice of reason to me throughout this long process.

To Chris, for hooking me up with my cover and also allowing me to annoy you with endless questions.

To Cindy, for saving me from throwing all of this away because I couldn't figure out how to format and design a book by myself.

Thank you to all of my friends and family, the Rinaldis, the Della Torres, and everyone else in my life for being there for me when I needed you. Thank you for listening to me talk about this book nonstop and for dealing with my constant badgering to read my stories over and over to make sure they were funny and worth publishing. Thanks especially to Maddy, Faith, Krissy, Lauren, Cathy, Chris B., Elliot, Cathy D. and Nate—I cannot thank you enough for being there for me and not telling me to go screw.

To my Gram, for just being you.

To Neil and Jen, for your never-ending love and support.

To Little Neil and Nick, for making me happy just by being you. I love you guys more than you know.

To the LaValle family, for letting me be "just one of the family" all of these years.

To my dad, for your love and support. Thank you for allowing me to write these funny stories about you without questioning any of it.

To my mom, who luckily gave me a whole lifetime's worth of love in the 10 short years I was blessed to have had her.

And lastly to Lynn, who left me with so many dysfunctional and funny life experiences to write this book about.

Love you all!

Made in the USA
Middletown, DE
04 May 2019